The
VOLUNTEER'S
Survival Manual

The
VOLUNTEER'S
Survival Manual

The
Only Practical Guide to
Giving Your Time and Money

Darcy Campion Devney

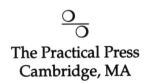

The Practical Press
Cambridge, MA

By the same author:
Organizing Special Events and Conferences:
A Practical Guide for Busy Volunteers and Staff

Published by: The Practical Press
P.O. Box 2296
Cambridge, MA 02238

Text ©1992 Darcy Campion Devney.
Cover and illustrations ©1992 Cassandra Boell.
Edited by Robert E. Devney.
Index by Jo-Ann MacElhiney.

Cataloging in Publication Data
Devney, Darcy Campion.   The Volunteer's survival manual: the only practical guide to giving your time and money / Darcy Campion Devney. p. cm. Includes bibliographical references and index. ISBN 0-9630686-9-5
1. Voluntarism — United States - Handbooks, manuals, etc. 2. Volunteers — Training of. 3. Charities — United States. 4. Consumer education — United States. I. Title.
HN49.V64   361.37 QBI91-1420
Library of Congress Catalog Card Number: 91-67573

Printed (on acid-free paper) and manufactured in the United States of America.

2   4   6   8   10   9   7   5   3   1

*This book is dedicated to
the preservation of an endangered species —
the happy volunteer.*

Contents

Part Three
Savvy Networking:
People and Politics

Part Four
What Do You Give,
What Do You Get?

Part Five
A Volunteer's Dilemmas:
Evaluations and Ethics

**Part Six
Resources**

Graphics

Lists

Introduction

The Volunteer's Survival Manual: The Only Practical Guide to Giving Your Time and Money is a consumer's handbook for volunteers.

A *consumer's* handbook? Well, if you wanted to buy a house and needed a book to help you with the decision, you'd look for a guide with sections on how to:

♦ Define your needs and resources
♦ Research and compare what's on the market
♦ Negotiate with the people involved and solve problems
♦ Understand the relevant financial transactions
♦ Learn about special circumstances in the industry

A book on volunteering should offer the same kinds of information, because volunteerism is very big business.

The total assets of philanthropic organizations — excluding religious institutions — are estimated at close to one-half trillion dollars. Gross receipts by the nonprofit sector represent almost 10% of the Gross National Product (GNP). An estimated 80 million Americans are volunteers and club members. They work on a variety of tasks for thousands of organizations. Almost 10% of the total hours worked by the U.S. labor force (equivalent to more than 10 million full-time jobs) is attributed to volunteers and staff members at nonprofit organizations.

Are you an informed, prepared volunteer? Are your contributions really making a difference to you and to those people and causes that you care about? Just as you shop around for a house or car, you must also seek out the best value for your volunteer hour and dollar.

As one long-time volunteer put it, "You need to be educated in *how* to be a volunteer . . . and what it *means* to be a volunteer."

What This Book Will Do for You

The Volunteer's Survival Manual: The Only Practical Guide to Giving Your Time and Money isn't a book about how volunteers can solve society's problems and heal the world, nor a directory of organizations who are in need of volunteers.

Whether you're searching for the right organization, or you're already heavily involved in a long-term volunteer position, *The Volunteer's Survival Manual* is an everyday handbook for volunteers. My "practical" approach means to be just that: a realistic guide to the nitty-gritty of contributing your time and money.

If you supervise volunteers or direct a corporate volunteer department, this book can be a vital resource in developing your program. If you teach a course in philanthropy or community service, this book can form the basis for a semester of discussion. For career and academic counselors, this book offers straightforward advice about student internships, volunteer credentials, and résumé enhancement.

The goal of *The Volunteer's Survival Manual* is to make you an informed, successful volunteer. After reading this book, you'll stop to think the next time you are asked to volunteer. And you'll have the resources to ask the right questions and make an informed decision.

Questions and Answers

The Volunteer's Survival Manual teaches you to handle every aspect of your volunteer memberships wisely.

> *"I'm interested in environmental issues. What is the best group for me to join?"*

> *"I think my husband spends too much time on his drama productions, and not enough on work. What can I do about it?"*

Whether you're just beginning your search for the right organization, or you're already committed to a specific one, an evaluation is the place to start. Part One, *Where Do You Fit? 1001 Ways to Volunteer*, shows you how to match your needs with a nonprofit organization. Choose the best one for you — and avoid spending time on the wrong one.

"I only want to volunteer one weekend a month, and I want to do something different every month. Is that possible?"

"For the past four years, I've drawn cartoons for my club's newsletter. Now that I'm going back to work, how do I use this experience to land a job in graphic arts?"

Do you want to pick the right volunteer job to suit your interests, or use your volunteer work to choose or change careers? Part Two, *Join Today, New Job Tomorrow: The Professional Approach,* teaches you to list and evaluate the full range of your volunteer commitments, and transfer skills to paid positions. Job descriptions for a range of volunteer positions are provided for your résumé. Gain respect for your volunteer work — and for yourself.

"My husband had a huge argument with the head of the bazaar committee, and now he wants to join a different church. How do I patch things up?"

"All the sessions at my association's annual conference were aimed at real beginners. I've been in the business for several years now, and I don't want my time wasted. Can I do anything to make sure things are different next year?"

Whether your argument is with people or their actions, "petty politics" is a frequent complaint from many volunteers. Part Three, *Savvy Networking: People and Politics,* demonstrates how to negotiate the obstacle course of personal relationships in nonprofit organizations — without falling flat on your face. And you get some handy advice about solving organizational problems, large and small.

"How do I know if the organization I'm contributing money to really uses it to benefit the homeless?"

"I never get noticed in my organization. Everyone else has an award except me. How can I get recognition?"

Maybe you realize that the homeless problem never seems to go away, or feel that your hard work just doesn't get rewarded. What are your time and money worth to your organization? Part Four, *What Do You Give, What Do You Get?* adds up *all* your contributions. Sift through the rhetoric. Are your total contributions balanced by benefits from your organization to you and to those people and causes that you care about — or are you being taken advantage of? And learn about the educational opportunities in your volunteer work.

> *"This is the fourth organization I've joined in two years. I never seem to find the right one. What should I do?"*

> *"A local pizza parlor has offered to buy jackets for the team if we agree to print the store logo on the back. Is this a good deal?"*

How do you know it's time to change your volunteer commitments — or refuse a volunteer opportunity outright? Is corporate charity a sham? In Part Five, *A Volunteer's Dilemmas: Evaluations and Ethics*, you can sample current controversies, and take a look at the future of your volunteer life.

Why I Wrote This Book

I have volunteered since kindergarten. Before I was thirteen, I was a Brownie, a Wavette, and a Girl Scout. As an adult, I joined groups as diverse as NAFE (National Association for Female Executives, a professional association) and SCA (Society for Creative Anachronism, a historical hobby group).

As a volunteer, I have:

- ◆ Organized special events.
- ◆ Chaired meetings.
- ◆ Written articles for newsletters.
- ◆ Taught classes.
- ◆ Counseled students on résumé-writing.
- ◆ Buttonholed people to sign petitions.
- ◆ Put plastic covers on library books.
- ◆ Sewn costumes.
- ◆ Pasted mailing labels on brochures.
- ◆ Passed out programs at plays.
- ◆ Taken minutes at meetings.
- ◆ Scrubbed pots.
- ◆ Chopped vegetables.
- ◆ Swept floors.
- – Plus various other tasks.

Some volunteer work actually led to my current profession.

With other members of a programming committee, I wrote a booklet for club members on how to plan fund-raisers. Afterwards, I wanted to know more. I began to investigate other organizations and to interview volunteers and professionals. Eventually all this led to my first published work, *Organizing Special Events and Conferences: A Practical Guide for Busy Volunteers and Staff.* (See *Resources*, or use the order form in the back of this book.)

As we head toward the 21st century, volunteering is being promoted in local and national media on a "do good, feel good" basis. Mainstream publications are rarely critical of nonprofit activities (though there was a brief flurry of negative press in the late 80s, when small businesses felt threatened by competition from nonprofits). Most of the publicity seems to me to be a form of advertisement by nonprofit organizations hoping for new volunteers and donors — and by governments hoping to cut costs.

"The nonprofit world is full of innovative, committed, hardworking people, but it is also troubled by waste, ineffective programs, flimflam, and distorted priorities," says a nonprofit expert. "Charities and foundations don't do a very good job of policing themselves. Very rarely do they publicly criticize or shun those groups involved in illegal or unethical behavior or take steps to insure that their peer organizations are providing the best quality of services possible." (*The Chronicle of Philanthropy*, August 13, 1991.)

I agree. Unlike any other big business, the nonprofit sector is subject to minimal examination. No federal agency exists to regulate nonprofit activities. Each year, the Internal Revenue Service (IRS) audits about 9,000 nonprofit organizations — and registers about 40,000 new ones. Most state agencies created to oversee nonprofits function primarily as data collectors.

What is missing, in my opinion, is the *customer's* viewpoint. As a lifelong volunteer, I wrote *The Volunteer's Survival Manual: The Only Practical Guide to Giving Your Time and Money* as a consumer's handbook to volunteering. Again, just as you shop around for a house or car, you must also seek out the best value for your volunteer hour and dollar.

Make your volunteer contributions count!

Part One

Where Do You Fit?
1,001 Ways to Volunteer

Chapter 1

The Right Thing to Do?
Look Before You Leap

As a typical joiner, you might be unaware of how much time and money you already give away. If someone asked, "Did you contribute to nonprofit organizations in the past year?" you might remember that you: agreed to payroll deduction (United Way); gave spare foreign coins to an airline attendant (UNICEF); paid membership dues (American Medical Association); got your car washed at the high school rally (Kennedy School); and bought a raffle ticket (St. Elizabeth's Hospital).

If you're really sharp, you might list goods as well as money: old eyeglasses to the Lions Club, outgrown clothing to the Salvation Army, used books for the yard sale at the Episcopal church.

And, of course, during the last year, you probably gave time and services, too. Perhaps you made centerpieces for a benefit banquet (American Diabetes Association), or staffed a table at the mall (League of Women Voters), or donated blood at a blood drive (American Red Cross).

What's Your Current Situation?

Let's take a snapshot of your current volunteer life. Summing up your hour and dollar contributions for the last year can be an eye-opener.

This evaluation takes an hour or two, but if you are reading this book, you probably spend more time than that volunteering each week. And an evaluation will help you gather information that will probably change your volunteer life. (It changed mine.)

Try sitting down with a good friend (maybe someone who's involved in the same organization, so you can jog each other's memory).

Collect three tools: your wallet or identification card file, your checkbook register, and your calendar for the last year. (See Graphic 1.1, *A Donor's Documents*.)

How Many Organizations Do You Belong To?

Open your wallet and list every membership card you carry.

Remember, hobby and interest groups can take up a large percentage of your leisure time. A 1988 Philip Morris survey found that one out of every five respondents had "served as an officer of some club or organization" within the previous 12 months.

Ten Review Questions

Do you:

♦ Belong to a professional association or union?

♦ Raise funds for public television?

♦ Play on your company's baseball league?

♦ Attend a church or temple?

♦ Buy tickets for the local museum?

♦ Participate in block associations?

♦ Sign nomination papers for political candidates?

♦ Support your child's involvement in drama club?

♦ Demonstrate for a social cause?

♦ Work on or contribute to capital campaigns for your *alma mater*?

How Much Time Do You Contribute?

Determining how much time you contribute to each organization is difficult, because usually time demands are irregular, depending on the season and the extent of certain projects.

Graphic 1.1 ♦ **A Donor's Documents**

Of course, many of your commitments may double as "social" occasions with other club members, and you may be reluctant to consider these as club-oriented contributions. If most of what you discuss is club business, however, count these hours.

The easiest method is to check your calendar for the last year.

Add up monthly business meetings, committee meetings, regularly scheduled sessions. If you paste up the newsletter every week or type and distribute the meeting minutes every month, you have a good idea of how many hours it takes. Don't forget one-time efforts: If you made 22 felt baskets for the Easter bazaar or if you picked up the football team uniforms, make a note. Include door-to-door canvassing or soliciting time, transportation time, telephone calls.

Estimate the total hours, and fill in the grand total on the chart. (See Graphic 1.2, *Where Does Your Time Go?*)

How Much Money Do You Contribute?

Now figure out how much money you gave to organizations in the last year.

Look at your checkbook, and add up banquet stubs, subscriptions, raffle tickets, and Girl Scout cookies. Don't forget membership fees and dues. Estimate transportation and supplies. If you are a regional officer and make a lot of long-distance phone calls, review your telephone bills to determine what percentage should be "charged" to your volunteer budget. Fill out the chart. (See Graphic 1.3, *Where Does Your Money Go?*)

"Isn't it tax-deductible?" Maybe. (See Chapter 7, *Money*.)

The Grand Total

If you've performed the above calculations honestly and diligently, I guarantee you're shocked at the amount of time and/or money you've given to various organizations.

Did you spend more money on your teenager's cheerleading than on your church, and do you wish it were the other way around? Did you find you were with members of your political issues group more frequently than with your spouse? If you find volunteer activities interfere with paid employment or family obligations, take this opportunity to reschedule to achieve a healthy balance.

Organization	Task	Number of hours		
		Weekly	Monthly	Other
Column subtotals				
		(x52)	(x12)	—
Totals				
Total hours/year				

Graphic 1.2 ♦ Where Does Your Time Go?

There is no hard-and-fast rule for minimum and maximum contributions to nonprofit organizations. According to a 1989 Gallup poll, volunteers contributed an average of 4 hours per week, and $1,022 per year.

- ♦ Traditional religious tithes run from 1% to 10% of your income. According to a 1991 study, members of 31 Protestant denominations gave an average of 2.64% of their disposable income to the church in 1989.
- ♦ "President and Mrs. Bush contributed a total of $38,667 to 50 charities last year. That works out to about 8.5% of their $452,732 income. Vice President and Mrs. Quayle gave $3,624 to charity — just under 3% of their income of $121,126." (*The NonProfit Times*, May, 1991.)
- ♦ The "fair share" standard used by one federated charity works out to about 1 hour's pay per month.
- ♦ The "Give Five" campaign sponsored by Independent Sector (a coalition of nonprofit organizations that are naturally interested in increasing volunteer activity) suggests that you volunteer 5 hours per week and 5% of your income "to a cause you believe in."

Common sense is mandatory here. Don't get talked into anything you don't want to do. (See Chapter 3, *Promises, Promises*.)

Be especially cautious when you are entering new territory — just moved, just started a new job, just became a parent. You are most vulnerable then to joining and contributing "just to belong."

Why Do You Want to Volunteer?

Being a volunteer is currently an approved activity in American society. You can spot a "hot" cause by the numbers of celebrity spokespersons and articles in the media. AIDS and homelessness are both causes that enjoyed peak popularity in the recent past.

"Frequently, volunteerism takes on a very altruistic aura. You are supposed to volunteer because you want to help others, and I do believe that is one of the reasons people volunteer," says Carolyn Losos, who has worked with a number of groups, including Leadership St. Louis, Parents as Teachers, and Girl Scouts of the USA.

Organization	Purpose	Amount donated		
		Monthly	Annual	Other
Column subtotals				
		(x12)	—	—
Totals				
Total $/year				

Graphic 1.3 ♦ Where Does Your Money Go?

However, she adds, "Maybe you volunteer because you would like to open up new friendships, or a new way of life, or find new interests. Many people volunteer, quite honestly, because they think that with volunteering comes power and the ability to network with people. There are lots of legitimate reasons to volunteer, and I don't think you should be ashamed of your reasons."

Eight Characters in Search of a Volunteer Role

+ Annie Activist — wants to change society
+ Diane Dogooder — wants to help someone less fortunate
+ Donald Debtor — wants to return the favor
+ Pam Professional — wants to further career plans
+ Sally Socialite — wants to meet people
+ Fred Funseeker — enjoys the activity
+ Cynthia Citizen — feels a sense of duty
+ Oliver Obedience — has been ordered to serve time

You Want to Change Society or Solve a Problem

Virginia McCullough, a Chicago writer, hopes that the groups she belongs to can make a difference. "I'm on the local political issues committee for the National Writer's Union. We're going to deal with censorship first. First Amendment issues really excite me, and the NWU gives me a natural place to be concerned about censorship. I belong to the American Civil Liberties Union, but the NWU is a natural environment in which to discuss and think about these issues."

Chapter Two, *Choosing and Joining*, teaches you to research organizations and make the most appropriate and effective choice.

You Want to Help Someone

President George Bush's view of volunteering includes one-on-one contact with the disadvantaged. "From now on in America, any definition of a successful life must include serving others."

You Want to Return the Favor

"A number of our volunteers are people who went through recovery programs — not necessarily this one. And some of our volunteers are former clients. Maybe they were here two years ago when they were out of work and needed a meal. Now that they have a job, they come back here to repay the favor," says Dave Schwartz, who works with addicts and homeless people in a rescue mission at CityTeam Ministries in San Jose, California.

It's Part of Your Career Plan

Susan Butler, a partner at Andersen Consulting, is clear about her motives. "One of the reasons why I wanted to be on the national board of the Girl Scouts of the USA is the skills that I was going to be able to learn. I knew I had a lot to contribute, because my background was different from the backgrounds of a lot of people on the board. But I also knew that I was going to gain experience."

Volunteer work may offer the chance to expand your professional repertoire. Apprentices can learn and develop skills while gaining recognition from business peers. (One writer had never done an audiovisual script, so she wrote one for her local zoo at no charge.)

Students can receive training or class credit as interns with nonprofit associations. "For one thing, I get a lot to put on my résumé," claims Sheryl Fitzgibbon, a student who is heavily involved with a professional association, "but that isn't why I do it. I do it because I enjoy interacting with people, I enjoy being involved, I enjoy my position as a leader."

In Part Two, *Join Today, New Job Tomorrow: The Professional Approach*, you'll find a hands-on guide to using your volunteer experience to give a boost to your career.

You Want to Meet People

As program director at a volunteer exchange, Joan Patterson is confident about social motivations for volunteer work. "For people who don't have a lot of friends, it's an opportunity to make some." Joining a club is frequently touted as the way for singles and lonely people to meet and make friends.

Part Three, *Savvy Networking: People and Politics*, can help you ease your way into comfortable relationships with other volunteers and staff of nonprofit organizations.

You Enjoy the Activity

Carolyn Neal, an administrative assistant, promises, "Volunteering puts balance in your life. Everyone needs an activity in their private time that is completely opposite to their professional life."

Part Four, *What Do You Give, What Do You Get?* encourages you to appreciate the intangible and tangible rewards of your volunteer work.

You Feel a Sense of Duty

"I never really thought about why I do this. It's part of my normal life, part of my social contract," says one volunteer. "I'm not just here to take, I'm on this earth to give something of service to my fellow human beings."

You Don't Want to, But —

Some volunteers aren't offered a choice; they are assigned by their boss, or union membership is a company requirement, or community service is a requirement of a school's curriculum. Judges sometimes sentence offenders to work in community service organizations.

Part Five, *A Volunteer's Dilemmas: Evaluations and Ethics*, discusses the nationwide trend toward "mandatory volunteering."

What Are Your Goals?

Your motives are probably mixed, and different for each organization. You can gain friends, status, training, and other benefits. You can fulfill cherished ideals, work for societal change, or satisfy a sense of duty.

You must be careful to choose your membership to suit *you*, not to suit the organization.

Ricki Wasserman supervises more than 200 volunteers at the Queens Borough Public Library in Jamaica, New York. She realizes that people may choose to work with the same organization for different reasons. "Our older volunteers seek both a social and a work climate as a bridge from career into retirement. Teenagers volunteer to fulfill community service requirements through either their schools or youth groups."

The unhappiest volunteer is one who belongs to the wrong organizations, for the wrong reasons, giving the wrong contributions in the wrong ways.

The best way to avoid overcommitment and ensure your satisfaction is to explore your motivations and the organization's aims.

Create specific *personal goals* for every membership. These goals can be minimal ("Receive and read the quarterly newsletter to stay informed on child welfare issues") or ambitious ("Use my position on the programming committee to meet five celebrities this year").

That's what this book is about — how to evaluate yourself, your organization, and your contributions, and make these decisions carefully.

Your volunteer time and money is the lifeblood of nonprofit organizations — give and get the best return on your investment!

Chapter 2

Choosing and Joining: Competition Between Nonprofits

As Clark Kent Ervin, associate director at the Office of National Service, observed, "We think we are at the crest of a wave here. The country is willing to engage in community service."

Organizations that have always relied on volunteers are expanding volunteer roles, and organizations that never used volunteers before have begun to rely on unpaid help. The cutbacks in government funding and the growth in the nonprofit sector (since 1967, the number of nonprofits has tripled — and the Internal Revenue Service (IRS) registers almost 40,000 new nonprofit organizations each year) have led to even more competition for volunteer hours and dollars.

Take advantage of that competition. Think of it as brand choices; do some comparison shopping among nonprofit organizations. (See Graphic 2.1, *Shopping for an Organization.*) Outline your preferences; select the organization that clicks for you.

Choose from Hundreds of Models

Suppose you are thinking of volunteer work with animals.

The American Society for the Prevention of Cruelty to Animals (ASPCA) is probably the first group that comes to mind, because it is the oldest humane society in America (founded in 1866).

Graphic 2.1 ◆ Shopping for an Organization

But it's not the only game in town.

Ask to see the Encyclopedia of Associations at your local library. Including the ASPCA, more than 75 groups claim to be involved in "animal welfare." Perhaps you are less concerned with pets, and more attracted by "wildlife conservation." If so, you have almost 100 groups to choose from, from Ducks Unlimited to the Elephant Interest Group. Or perhaps your interests are more in line with the National Audubon Society or the other 96 groups who define their area simply as "conservation."

Okay, you've narrowed your area to "animal welfare." Take a quick look at the listings. All of these groups are competing for *your* time and money.

If you want to join a large organization, the Humane Society of the United States boasts 975,000 members.

In 1951, the Animal Welfare Institute (AWI) was established by people concerned about treatment of lab animals and animals raised for food, about trapping methods, and about endangered species. Save the Whales is one of the AWI's projects.

Maybe you prefer hands-on involvement. If you're fond of horses and live in the right part of Texas, you might consider moseying over to the Fund for Animals' Black Beauty Farm for homeless and abused horses. Or if you prefer dogs and live near Walton, New York, the Peace Plantation animal sanctuary of the National Humane Education Society may collar your attention.

If your child reads the *KIND News* newspaper at school, you're already involved with the National Association for Humane and Environmental Education (NAHEE). People for the Ethical Treatment of Animals (PETA) is a relatively new group (formed in 1980) that "opposes all forms of animal exploitation." Perhaps you can combine two interests, and join Concern for Helping Animals in Israel (CHAI). Or, because of your professional status, Psychologists for the Ethical Treatment of Animals (PsyETA) may be the right group for you.

Obviously, animal lovers enjoy a wide range of choices. But even highly specialized interests offer variety. If you are a Star Trek fan, you can choose to beam aboard any of five different groups: The Federation Council; Star Trek: The Official Fan Club; Star Trek Welcommittee; Starfleet; and Trekville USA.

They Want You

Nonprofit organizations rely on you — the volunteer — and they employ a number of means to get your attention and support. "Organizations have to spend more time and money on volunteers today," says Joyce Hatton Yarrow, president of the Institute for Nonprofit Training and Development.

Various publications list volunteer opportunities (usually divided into issues, such as the environment, homelessness, etc.). (See *Resources.*) Or start with the Volunteer Bureau, Center, or Exchange in your area. (Look in the *Yellow Pages.*) Joan Patterson, program director at the Volunteer Exchange in San Jose, California, notes, "Last year, the number of people who looked us up in the phone book doubled."

At the Learning Connection in Providence, Rhode Island, a spokesperson from Volunteers in Action presents a course called "Rhode Island's Volunteer Options." The adult education center in your community might be following suit.

A school in Maryland puts a detailed list of "volunteer opportunities" — including tasks and dates for special events — right on the student information form that parents receive when enrolling their children.

And a theater company in Massachusetts uses a sophisticated approach, touting "starring roles for volunteers," and promising, "You'll use leadership skills that will help you as you climb the corporate ladder of success."

If you are wealthy, you may be formally courted by organizations who want your financial support. Otherwise, your initial contact with an organization is likely to be fairly casual, possibly through a friend. Maybe you attended a special open-to-the-public event, or bought a product, or signed a petition — presto, you were added to the mailing list.

Employee volunteer programs are growing, too; in the last five years, the number of corporations that sponsored formal employee/retiree volunteer programs increased from 600 to 900. Maybe your company maintains listings of volunteer opportunities in your community.

In organizations such as Business Volunteers for the Arts and Retired Senior Volunteers, you are originally lent out to a specific organization, and you may end up volunteering directly with that organization. According to Martin B. Cominsky, director of Business Volunteers for the Arts, USA, 40 percent of volunteers eventually wind up on the boards of directors of their assigned groups.

Many organizations (e.g., alumni, honors, community) automatically consider you a member without any encouragement or permission from you. Remember: you can say "no" to such automatic memberships.

The Sherlock Holmes Approach

Taking your motivations and the organization's stated objectives into account, select no more than five organizations for consideration.

Before choosing an organization (or when evaluating current memberships), you should find out everything you can about it. (See Graphic 2.2, *The Sherlock Holmes Approach.*)

If your target organizations combat illiteracy, for example, you want to know:

+ *Who* (Are the tutors mostly middle-class liberals?)
+ *What* (Does the organization concentrate on lobbying education officials or setting up programs in schools?)
+ *How much* (What percentage of each contribution is spent on administration?)
+ *Where* (Are the majority of the students children from low-income families throughout the state, or adult foreigners in your town?)

Researching an Organization
+ Meet members.
+ Browse through the newsletter.
+ Read official documents.
+ Ask awkward questions.
+ Analyze the budget.
+ Review membership categories.

Graphic 2.2 ♦ The Sherlock Holmes Approach

Time spent researching an organization now will save your joining or contributing to the wrong organization. And sometimes the investment is minimal; a quick once-over of a club's newsletter, for example, will often show that it's not the group for you.

Most important, be on the lookout for things that don't match up: Does the organization do what it says it does?

Meet Members

Ask for a profile of members, so you can imagine how you would fit in. Don't just assume that everyone in the group must be like your friend who's asking you to join.

Attend a seminar, a board or committee meeting; or shadow a volunteer during working time.

Tip: If most officers are holding down at least two offices, the group may be dominated by an "inner circle" — or perhaps only a few people do most of the work, and the rest of the members coast on their efforts.

Browse Through the Newsletter

Read recent issues of the newsletters, both local and national. Develop a sense of the organization's philosophy and goals.

Read Official Documents

Ask for the *annual report* and the *articles of incorporation* (sometimes called a *charter* or *constitution*). These documents give you an invaluable glimpse into the corporate structure.

If you've been active in an organization for some time, request this paperwork. You may be surprised by how your organization (or your concept of your organization) differs from its actual legal entity.

Ask about voting rights. For example, you may think that you are entitled to an equal vote in all disputes, but your organization can be structured in a way that doesn't allow members any participation in policy decisions.

Ask about mailing list sales. (See Chapter 8, *Volunteer Value.*)

And find out about liability insurance — a hot topic for today's volunteers. (See Chapter 3, *Promises, Promises.*)

Inspecting a Newsletter

♦ What is emphasized?

♦ Is there a list of accomplishments for the past year?

♦ Are volunteers in action prominently featured?

♦ Is the attitude friendly or formal?

♦ Are next year's projects already in the planning stages?

♦ Is it bilingual?

♦ Are rich donors mentioned?

♦ What project or committee gets the most space?

♦ Are the people pictured ethnically diverse?

♦ Do the same people appear in all the pictures? (Again, this could indicate an inner circle attitude.)

Ask Awkward Questions

What is the primary purpose of the organization, and how does the organization work toward its goals? A local theatre group, for example, performs many functions: professional (training new actors and technical staff); social (getting members to know each other); and educational (teaching drama to members and audience).

Do not be surprised if you discover that an organization's purported or original purpose is not what the group is focused on currently. Organizations have a natural life cycle.

Do you think it's more important to work for reform of the government's housing policy (social action), or to work in a homeless shelter (social service)?

Perhaps it's one of the new cause-of-the-month clubs, such as Community Impact (in which members are mostly young professionals, who select short-term projects from a variety of popular causes). Why aren't the volunteers working with a specific cause permanently? Is the group really just a cover for networking or dating purposes? Or are the members easily bored? And how does the group evaluate and choose "worthy" causes?

If the organization was started (as many are) as a splinter group of another organization, find out when and *why* the split occurred. Was the split the result of an organizational dispute, with the "losers" quitting to begin their own group? How do you feel about the issue at dispute? Or did the group come into being because someone wanted to be important? (See Chapter 10, *The Volunteer Track*, for more discussion of creating a new group.)

When checking out professional groups, find out about the certification process. Is it automatic? To prove how easy it is to get accreditation from some groups, one sceptic enrolled his cat as a member of a national professional association. (When the sceptic subsequently publicized the cat's new status, the organization cancelled the membership and sued.) (See Chapter 5, *Relationships*, for more advice on choosing a professional association.)

Analyze the Budget

Read the organization's annual budget line by line. (Organizations with an annual income of over $100,000 should be able to give you an audited financial statement.)

Budgets reveal what the organization considers important or unimportant. The project with the most funding is the most significant activity, and probably consumes the most time and effort. Fund-raising expenses should be less than one-third of the total expenses. If more, find out why.

Beware. Fund-raising expenses can be made to look artificially small: Tucked into a fund-raising packet, a paragraph about the "seven warning signs of such-and-such disease" can allow the cost of the whole packet to be counted as education, not fund-raising. Compare what fund-raising letters *say* about the distribution of funds with what the budget actually *shows*.

Looking at income sources tells you how much fund-raising the organization does (and will, therefore, expect from you). Compare the current year to the previous year. Has the focus of the organization changed? Did membership fees rise steeply? If so, where did the new income go?

What percentage of contributions is spent on membership services, such as newsletters, meetings, and libraries? How much on salaries? How many officers are paid — and which important positions are unpaid?

Category	Dues	Voting	Hold office	Notes
Life	no	yes	yes	reward for outstanding service or donation
Honorary	no	no	no	served with distinction or important in field
Active	yes	yes	yes	typical member; largest category
Junior	discount	no	yes, local	limited period; usually students
Associate	discount	no	no	often spouse or child of an active member
Nonresident	discount	no	no	residence remote from activities; e.g., foreign
Informal	no	no	no	often a one-time effort or event

Graphic 2.3   ♦   Typical Membership Categories

Check with the agency in your state that oversees the activities of charitable organizations (in Pennsylvania, for example, it's called the Charitable Organizations Commission). Three national nongovernmental organizations set standards for public charities, and prepare research reports on individual organizations: the National Charities Information Bureau (NCIB), the Philanthropic Advisory Service (PAS) of the Council of Better Business Bureaus, and The Other Side. (See *Resources*.)

Review Membership Categories

Membership categories are usually determined by some mixture of financial support, service contribution, geographic location, and family lifestyle. Make sure that the category you choose matches the level of involvement and commitment you want. (See Graphic 2.3, *Typical Membership Categories*.)

Many volunteer members don't look before they leap.

Spending several hours at this stage to investigate your short list of organizations (calling monitoring agencies, meeting members, reading official documents and newsletters, and attending meetings) ensures that you pick the right organization for you — or quit the organization that's wrong for you.

Part Two

Join Today,
New Job Tomorrow:
The Professional Approach

Chapter 3

Promises, Promises: Volunteer Opportunities

"One of our success stories is Michael Mitchell, who began his career as an intern at my company back in 1981," says Michael Levine, president of Levine/Schneider Public Relations in Los Angeles, California. "Michael was willing to work long days and do the grunt work — stuff envelopes, answer phones — but he was also given an opportunity to sit in on interviews, attend press functions, and grasp the public relations business from the ground up. Within a short time he was made a paid junior publicist. When he left my company four years later he was tour press director, and today he is Vice President of Publicity at Motown Records. He has told me that interning gave him the broad insight that led him to his current position."

Whether you view volunteer work solely as a tool for career advancement, as your best chance to make friends, or simply as a way of doing your part to help others, choose your volunteer position carefully.

"Most good agencies use volunteer applications," according to one United Way volunteer. "Not all, but most." Don't be surprised to be handed a form that closely resembles a job application. (See Graphic 3.1, *Volunteer Application*.)

Design Your Own Job

"In general, potential volunteers are allowed more leeway in determining what kind of job they do than they think. Volunteer directors are often willing to custom-make a position for a specific volunteer," observes Patrick Shannon, director of volunteer services at the University of Chicago Hospitals. "People come in who want to be patient visitors with a certain category of patient — Hispanics, or people with AIDS, whatever — and I'm able to set that up."

To outline your own ideal volunteer opportunity, begin with three questions:

♦ What do you want to do?

♦ When do you want to do it?

♦ Where do you want to do it?

What Do You Want to Do?

In her position as program director at a Volunteer Exchange, Joan Patterson has found that "Volunteering can be a great opportunity to take risks — you would never get a paid job that would let you do some of the work you are given an opportunity to do as a volunteer." Take a chance; experiment with something new.

But you must be sure that whatever you pick sparks your interest. In *Beyond Success* (see *Resources*), the authors ask some pointed questions: "When you have the radio on in the kitchen, which news stories make you turn off the running water? When you're reading the newspaper, which articles make you talk to yourself? Ask your friends what topics you complain about most."

"Sometimes a nurse wants to do something to take advantage of her nursing skill; sometimes she wants to do something completely different," explains Betty Baker, who donates her time to the Voluntary Action Center in Boston, Massachusetts.

If you're interested in donating your professional skills (even after retirement), perhaps your trade group organizes *pro bono* services. For example, many of the American Optometric Association's members provide free eye examinations to uninsured low-income workers as part of the Vision USA program. And veterinarians throughout America donate their skills to the Friends of Animals' Breeding Control Program.

Name ——————————————————————————

Address ——————————————————————————

——————————————————————————

—————————————————— Phone —————— (night)

Occupation ——————————————————————

Business address ————————————————————

——————————————————————————

—————————————————— Phone —————— (day)

How did you hear about this organization? ——————

——————————————————————————

Why do you want to volunteer? ——————————

——————————————————————————

——————————————————————————

What would you like to do? ————————————

——————————————————————————

——————————————————————————

What experience have you had? ——————————

——————————————————————————

Skills (e.g., office, computer skills; foreign languages)

——————————————————————————

Education ————————————————————————

——————————————————————————

Geographic area preferred ——————————————

——————————————————————————

Transportation ——————————————————————

What hours are you available?

Mon	Tues	Wed	Thurs	Fri	Sat	Sun

In case of emergency, please notify ————————————

Address ——————————————————————————

——————————————————————————

—————————————————— Phone ————————

(Attach résumé if possible.)

Graphic 3.1 ♦ Volunteer Application

You can learn or practice almost any skill with an eye to your future career plans. For example, if you want to help feed the hungry, you can:

- Drive a truck to pick up and deliver foodstuffs
  (profession: truck, bus, or cab driver)
- Persuade supermarkets and restaurants to donate food
  (profession: administrator, grants writer)
- Package foods, pack trucks
  (profession: bagger in grocery store, mover)
- Cook and serve meals
  (profession: caterer, server, food service worker)
- Fix broken appliances and trucks
  (profession: repairperson, mechanic)
- Write letters to elected politicians to change policies
  (profession: lobbyist, writer)
- Organize benefit ball and community meetings
  (profession: meeting manager, special events planner)
- Fold, stamp, and mail brochures and fund-raising letters
  (profession: secretary, clerk)
- Entertain during a meal in a cafeteria
  (profession: performer, emcee)

When Do You Want to Do It?

First, determine how many hours you want to donate. The job descriptions in Chapter 4, *Your Résumé*, include an estimate of the number of hours a position would require in a mid-size city's local branch of a national organization. You can choose daily, weekly, monthly, quarterly, seasonal, occasional, or annual schedules — and any number of hours.

Some corporations, including Xerox and IBM, offer innovative "social leave" programs that give employees long-term leave to pursue volunteer opportunities.

Bea Scott, a retired head sales clerk, volunteers 8:15–10:15 a.m., six days a week, at a convalescent hospital in Mountain View, California.

Another California volunteer who specializes in raising funds for cultural institutions estimates, "For the symphony, I sit down about twice a month with one of the professionals, and we make calls and set appointments. Then we go out to the meetings. I spend about 10 hours each week."

Hyatt Hotels Corporation makes it easy for their managerial employees. Every manager may take one paid day each quarter to volunteer with the organization(s) of the individual hotel's choice.

The group 20/20 asks for $20 per year and 20 minutes per month.

"Winter Texans" in the Rio Grande Valley are involved in a variety of community projects during their seasonal vacations, from gleaning crops to leading tours.

Subscribe to *Volunteer Vacations Update* to find out about short-term efforts, such as a week clearing trails for the Appalachian Mountain Club. Or, if you're a student, contact Break Away for information on "alternative spring breaks." (See *Resources*.)

Or perhaps you could join Community Impact in San Francisco, where groups of about 30 young professionals work on a different project one weekend day each month.

And a variety of volunteer activities — walkathons, demonstrations, etc. — call for a one-time effort.

Where Do You Want to Do It?

Lelia Fykes-Ridley tried to decide, prior to retiring, how she would volunteer. "I didn't want to just sit home and do nothing. So I looked around at places I would enjoy. The zoo is wonderful in the summer, but not in the winter, so that's why I don't volunteer there. I went to other museums, but they didn't offer what I wanted." Fykes-Ridley settled on a volunteer position at Chicago's Museum of Science and Industry. "I've always enjoyed this museum. This is an interesting place; and it's rewarding when you see the little ones' eyes light up."

Go to your choice of volunteering and walk through it. Take a look, see what "feel" you get from being there.

What Are Your Responsibilities?

As a volunteer, you owe it to yourself, your organization, and your cause to behave responsibly. The following list may seem obvious, but a surprising number of volunteers feel entitled to show up late or not at all; to do sloppy good-enough work; or to procrastinate past deadlines. What a waste of time for you and for the organization!

Your Volunteer Responsibilities

- Pay dues.
- Attend meetings.
- Be punctual.
- Keep accurate records, financial and otherwise.
- Be supportive, loyal, enthusiastic.
- Keep informed on policies and procedures.
- Question, but accept majority decisions.
- Complete jobs you accept.
- Be friendly to new members.
- Maintain your balance; don't get overinvolved.

While most nonprofit organizations give volunteers a lot of leeway — and many volunteers learn on the job — a volunteer who expects to be treated professionally must behave professionally.

Stealing for a Good Cause Is Still Stealing

The photocopier at your paid job is not a free photocopier. You are doing a disservice to all when, without permission, you use supplies or time at your paid job for volunteer activities.

Suppose you are the newsletter editor for a neighborhood association. Each month, you use the photocopier at your paid job at the insurance company to make 100 copies of the newsletter for distribution to members. You are stealing supplies and machine use from your employer, *and* making it harder for the next newsletter editor, who won't be able to produce the newsletter on the same budget.

Instead, ask if the company is willing to donate the paper and photocopying, or not charge for photocopier use if your nonprofit organization supplies the paper. Offer to use the photocopier off-hours or weekends, so you don't slow down office work.

Put It in Writing

Undervaluing your volunteer experience is sadly typical, unless you are donating your professional skills. (See Chapter 8, *Volunteer Value*, to learn how your nonmonetary contributions add up.) Virginia McCullough, who volunteers her public relations services to Chicago-area nonprofit organizations, declares, "I consider that I am offering them high-class, professional skills that took me 16 years to learn."

Research the real-world paid job description, and you quickly gain respect for your contribution of labor.

Job Description Elements

- Job or office title, committee, or special project
- Purpose, importance to program goals
- Term of office, appointed or elected by
- Report to/supervised by/supervises
- Amount of salary if job were paid, scheduled hours
- Description of specific responsibilities
- Areas of responsibility (include geographic areas, budget, number of volunteers and staff)
- Reports prepared/other records kept
- Equipment used, (office) machines operated
- Award/promotion system
- Evaluation schedule and features
- Working conditions
- Qualifications/special qualifications
- Training requirements
- Organizational chart

A businessman told a student government volunteer that their duties were similar. And the student appreciates that. "It's really good experience. I'm sitting on the board of directors of a $3 million corporation, while I'm still in college. And I will definitely point that out in job interviews."

Carolyn Neal, former assistant to Congressman Michael D. Barnes, urges, "Put it on your résumé. I got my first job with a Congressional office by convincing them that my leadership skills from my volunteer experience were relevant." As a résumé/job interview tool, a description presents your contributions in a format that your prospective employer understands.

An organizational chart is always part of a complete job description; show where you and other volunteers and staff fit.

Do I Really Need a Contract?

A volunteer contract is a formal document between you and the organization; it is especially important if you intend to use your volunteer experience to secure a paid position. Think in terms of the legal notion of a contract: You are exchanging something of value with the organization (your time and energy for a job recommendation, or your expertise for a portfolio piece, etc.).

And benefits may be spelled out; for example, the volunteer contracts from the Fish and Wildlife Service, Park Service, or Forest Service divisions of government promise that volunteers are covered by workmen's compensation and liability insurance.

Your contract must include a schedule of evaluation meetings (at least twice a year). (See Graphic 3.2, *Volunteer Contract*.)

Can You Measure Success?

Joan Patterson, who works with volunteers every day, is convinced: "I think a volunteer should be treated like a staff member. I am a real advocate for having a job description, a contract, training, and orientation. Volunteers deserve to be evaluated and to evaluate the program."

And, she points out, evaluation can be a boon for the organization, as well. "We've gotten great ideas on how we can make the program better. It's worth it to include an evaluation." (See Graphic 3.3, *Volunteer Evaluation*.)

List the benchmarks by which you will be measured.

If you edit the newsletter, for example, you could track your progress with circulation figures (quantity goals), budget figures (financial goals), production schedules (time goals), or letters to the editor (quality goals).

Name _____

Address _____

_____

_____

Phone _____ (day) _____ (night)

Job title _____

Brief job description _____

_____

_____

_____

(Attach complete job description to this form.)

Period covered by agreement _____

Schedule _____

_____ Minimum hrs./month _____

I understand that I will not receive any compensation for the above work. Either party may cancel this agreement (at any time after the initial 3-month trial period) by notifying the other party. I hereby volunteer my services as described.

_____   _____
Signature of volunteer   Date

The organization agrees, while this arrangement is in effect, to provide such materials, equipment, and facilities as are available and needed to perform the work described above. Training and evaluation will be provided as specified in the attached job description. The organization will consider you as an employee only for the purpose of tort claims and compensation for work-related injuries.

_____   _____
Signature of organization official   Date

Graphic 3.2 ♦ Volunteer Contract

If you organize a special event, at a minimum use attendance records to judge success or failure (if it's a fund-raising event, compare your profit figures with those for previous years).

Be sure you are evaluated on your work, *not* the organization's; for example, did you and every other volunteer sell fewer tickets than ever before because the play was not a popular one?

Always keep accurate records of your participation (number of hours, description of projects, outline of tasks), and convince the organization to keep corresponding files.

As a student working for academic credit, you are usually asked to keep a journal of your volunteer time and tasks, as well as to produce papers or reports.

What About Recommendation Letters?

One of the best forms of feedback, especially for major projects, is a personal letter of recommendation. Of course, you expect and need these as a volunteer member; so, be sure to willingly write detailed ones as a supervisor. Event managers and chapter presidents are most frequently asked for letters of recommendation.

The letter of recommendation should be as much like a business letter of recommendation as possible. Include your name and organization office, the volunteer member's name and organization office, an abbreviated job description, the length of the job, and the number of years the person has been involved with the organization. Don't forget to explain the organization's purpose (if it might be unclear to nonmembers), and any objective and subjective evaluations of the volunteer member's work. (See Graphic 3.4, *Letter of Recommendation*.) Keep a photocopy for yourself and for the organization's files.

R-E-S-P-E-C-T

"Treat your volunteers like gold," urges a volunteer who supervised other volunteers during a political campaign. "They aren't paid staff; they don't have to be there."

When you are contributing your time, effort, and expertise, the organization is obliged to respect your rights as a worker. Remember that volunteer workers, in most situations, are not covered by the Fair Labor Standards Act.

Name _____

Address _____

_____

Phone _____ (day) _____ (night)

Job title _____

Period covered by this evaluation _____

Schedule _____

Categories	Great	Good	Fair	Poor
Quality of work				
Productivity				
Planning/organization				
Supervisory skills				
Relationships				
Dependability				
Initiative/motivation				
Technical ability				
Decision-making				
Adaptability				
Overall rating				

Supervisor's summary comments _____

_____

_____

_____

Supervisor's name _____ Date _____

Supervisor's signature _____

Date of next scheduled evaluation _____

Goals for next evaluation period _____

_____

_____

_____

(Attach complete job description to this form.)

Graphic 3.3 ♦ Volunteer Evaluation

Your Volunteer Rights

♦ Honesty	♦ Information
♦ Variety	♦ Supervision
♦ Training	♦ Consistency
♦ Staff rights	♦ Evaluation
♦ References	♦ Insurance

The easiest way to determine if you are being treated fairly is to ask if you are being treated at least as well as paid staff of the organization. For example, if the staff has a lounge room (for snacks or breaks), volunteers should be entitled to use that room or a similar room for volunteers only.

Who Does What?

"It used to be that just men were on the executive boards," says Susan Butler, now a veteran board member. "I think that's changing." However, womens' auxiliaries of fraternal organizations are still sometimes responsible for the brunt of the fund-raising, but unable to enjoy full membership.

If you are a woman, you may decide to boycott certain volunteer jobs entirely, such as making and serving coffee for staff meetings.

Or you may take the view of one former volunteer that it isn't the duty that matters, it's the company. "I do not mind stuffing envelopes. But I want to see some guys next to me stuffing them, too."

And learn to expect some power struggles with staff, especially in long-term assignments.

Can You Be Sued?

As a parent, you offer to drive a group of boys to an overnight camping area. An automobile accident kills you and one of your adolescent passengers and wounds several others. Can your estate be held liable for damages? Yes, in many states.

Disadvantaged Youth Center
200 South Street, Dallas, TX 00022

April 3, 1992

To Whom It May Concern:

I would like to offer my strongest recommendation for a volunteer of ours, Joshua Knight. Mr. Knight has proven himself to be a very intelligent and reliable volunteer at the Disadvantaged Youth Center. (The Center was established fifteen years ago, to provide a gathering place for children in the Roseville area. We run several programs, including some very successful sport teams, an after-school study group, and drug- and alcohol-free weekend dances.)

Shortly after he moved to our neighborhood five years ago, Mr. Knight signed up on the budget committee for a two-year stint. Mr. Knight has a good grasp of financial planning, so he put our finances in order, creating and maintaining budget books (our annual budget is $95,000). He has helped the programming committee with planning several fund-raisers, and has a keen eye for tax problems.

In 1990, he became a valuable member of the facilities committee, and is currently chairperson. He is a genius at scheduling space and dealing with conflicting demands. His latest challenge is spearheading the plans for a community garden.

I am sure that Joshua Knight would be an excellent addition to your company.

Sincerely,

Mr. Former Volunteer
Director, Volunteer Program

Graphic 3.4 ♦ Letter of Recommendation

Suppose you are the event manager for your club's annual Easter fair, and a guest is stricken with food poisoning. The guest sues the volunteer baker, your organization, and yourself. Are you legally responsible? Yes, if you haven't taken precautions.

"Every state now has a law pertaining specifically to legal liability of at least some types of volunteers. But according to the Nonprofits' Risk Management and Insurance Institute, all this legislation has contributed to a false impression that volunteers nationwide are immune from suit. To the contrary, says the Institute, most volunteers in most states remain fully liable for any harm they cause, and all volunteers remain liable for some actions. Only about half the states protect volunteers other than directors and officers." (*Nonprofit World*, January/February 1991.)

The Volunteer Protection Act (S. 1343) has not yet been passed, and, in any case, does not cover volunteers driving vehicles. The best protection against such difficulties is adequate insurance.

Before you become a legal representative (signing contracts for performers, caterers, vendors) or provide services (first aid, for example) or equipment (lending your grill or lawnmower), make sure the organization and your activities are covered. Get an agreement in writing if you can.

If you are organizing a special event, consider asking the organization to purchase event-specific one-time liability insurance. For a small Easter fair, such a policy could probably be purchased for under $1,000 (expensive, but worth it for the peace of mind).

Remember, however, that most insurance does *not* protect you if negligence or recklessness is proved.

Chapter 4

Your Résumé: Your Volunteer Experience at Work

For four years, Mark Olson concentrated on planning a single convention. He negotiated 3,400 hotel rooms in a big city, directed the efforts of more than 1,000 volunteers, scheduled more than 800 panels and lectures, and signed up 240 exhibitors.

In roughly the same time frame, for a different convention, Terry Phinney negotiated 1,000 hotel rooms, scheduled about 100 panels and lectures, directed the efforts of more than 100 volunteers, and signed up 140 exhibitors.

What is the difference between these two meeting managers?

Olson received *no pay* for his efforts — he was the volunteer chairperson for a science fiction convention. But Phinney was a *salaried* executive director for the American Camping Association.

"The management skills that a volunteer can develop are unbelievable. You can work on projects that you would never get a chance at otherwise," enthuses Susan Butler, who has demonstrated her expertise on the boards of Youth in Philanthropy and Girl Scouts of the USA. And Carolyn Losos, another veteran volunteer, agrees. "I know people whose lives changed because of opportunities that were a direct result of their volunteer involvement."

Putting your volunteer experience on your résumé is not just smart, it is your *right*.

Insist that your volunteer experience be seriously considered. If necessary, quote the United States Congress: ". . . experience in volunteer work should be taken into account by the Federal Government, State, and local governments, charitable and service organizations and private employers in the consideration of applicants for employment, and . . . provisions should be made for a listing and description of volunteer work on employment application forms." (Concurrent Resolution # 61, *Volunteers and the Importance of Volunteering*, August, 1988.)

What Counts?

According to the NATIONAL Volunteer Center, "Major companies that have already adopted policies and/or procedures to give equal consideration for volunteer experience include: TRW, United Airlines, AT&T, Coca-Cola, Levi Strauss & Company, and the Marriott Corporation."

Sometimes just the fact that you have volunteered, not the specific work itself, makes a difference when applying for jobs.

As Donald W. Davis, chairman of the board at Stanley Works, says, "A Stanley interviewer would be very much predisposed to people who were doing volunteer work, because it shows a side of their character — a value system — that is important to us. Not necessarily the experience they've gained by it, as the fact they did it. They were willing to spend their time at a volunteer activity that they thought was important. It would weigh heavily with us; we would consider it a real plus."

Suggestions for Your Résumé

When you draft your résumé, list all your volunteer experience. Being complete is more important than being concise. However, when you work on the final version, if you are trying to use volunteer experience to get a paying job, be as brief and businesslike as possible when you transfer the information to your résumé.

As an expert, you will sometimes be asked to *donate* your paid professional skills (usually on a one-time or limited basis). If you are in training, research or interview your paid counterparts, and base your job description on theirs.

Explain the purpose, size, and scope of the organization if it is not well-known — don't just use an acronym and expect the reader to recognize the group.

Unfortunately, listing certain controversial organizations can work against you. Don't list an organization if you aren't comfortable with prospective employers' assuming your sexual, racial, or political orientation from such association. Or purposely *include* such affiliations on your résumé — on the theory that you don't want to work for companies that show negative responses to such designations.

Use *quantities* as often as possible: "supervised 15 volunteers"; "raised $10,000 in two months"; "edited and produced monthly newsletter for 400 subscribers." Is your volunteer job equivalent to a full-time, part-time, or quarter-time job? Add up the hours, and put this figure on your résumé, too.

Job descriptions for common volunteer jobs start on the next page. The box at the bottom of each page suggests typical phrases for your résumé (most descriptions are applicable for local, regional, or national positions). Attach samples of your work to the résumé or offer to show your portfolio, if applicable.

Board Member

A board membership or chapter presidency is the most prestigious membership position, probably because you are very much in the public eye. This is also the office where you can make the most difference in how the organization is run, and how the organization is perceived by nonmembers.

If you are interested in business contacts and networking, this is the perfect slot.

Qualifications: A steady temper, a healthy pocketbook, and some experience in other nonprofit organizations are a good start for this position.

Career Path: Unless your financial support of the organization is considerable, you must earn a board membership by hard work. In order to serve on a local board, you should have been a local officer, or worked on a special project or committee for at least a year. Volunteers sometimes alternate between a chapter presidency and a board position (or sometimes combine the two).

Schedule: You attend board meetings, probably once a month for 2 to 3 hours. The smart board member reads the agenda and does an hour of research and calling around *before* the meeting, so as not to waste time. Board members are usually expected to attend most special events.

If you take on extra projects, you give more than 10 hours per month.

Board Member (Résumé Items)

♦ Researched and reviewed committee decisions.
♦ Formulated organizational goals.
♦ Monitored issues.
♦ Made policy.
♦ Chaired committee meetings.
♦ Solicited contributions.

Chapter President or Chair

The chapter president runs the group on a local level, and is frequently the legal representative of the organization. Although your vice presidents will handle subsections (finance, recruitment, etc.), you may put in extra work on problem areas.

Qualifications: The ability to see both sides of an issue, a likeable personality, and no overwhelming vested interest in a specific aspect of the organization all stand you in good stead for this job.

Career Path: You are more effective if you have held more than one local office, and worked on a special project or committee. A year as vice president can be a good training ground.

Schedule: You run meetings, probably once a month for 2 to 3 hours. Phone calls and paperwork may add another 2 hours each week. Keeping informal tags on committees and volunteers includes sitting in on other meetings (another 5 or 6 hours a month). You should also try to attend all local events, and possibly travel to some regional conferences.

Expect an investment of 8 to 12 hours per week, depending on how conscientious you are — and how much paperwork your organization requires.

Chapter President (Résumé Items)

- Chaired business and committee meetings.
- Wrote reports to regional and national officers.
- Monitored issues.
- Encouraged and directed programming for events.
- Participated in recruiting activities.
- Contributed to publications.
- Presided over award ceremonies.
- Attended events, practices, meetings.
- Maintained good contact with members.

Docent/Tour Guide

This is probably the most common volunteer job in museums. Working with members of the public on a regular basis gives you poise and self-confidence. You may physically lead tours around the museum, or present lectures and demonstrations for special exhibits, or work one-on-one with children or foreign visitors.

Qualifications: If you are fascinated by the museum's subject of study, your enthusiasm enables you to spark other people's interest.

Career Path: In some areas, considerable financial support of the organization and long hours working on fund-raising events are prerequisites, because the job is considered very prestigious.   In other areas, anyone who offers to spend a few hours being trained can choose this as their first volunteer position. After a year or so, you could transfer your people skills to a position as publicist or volunteer coordinator.

Schedule: You can count on a fixed schedule. After the initial training period, settle on a set number of tours (usually daytime, weekend). Sometimes you can be assigned to teach during daytime school tours. Hours can vary widely, depending on whether you volunteer once a month for a morning or a full day every weekend.

Docent/Tour Guide (Résumé Items)

- ◆ Kept current in fields of interest.
- ◆ Researched recent acquisitions.
- ◆ Conducted tours and answered questions.
- ◆ Greeted and guided guests and visitors.
- ◆ Developed new tours and presentations.

Event Manager

If you don't burn out, event or meeting management offers great opportunities to gain supervisory experience while being creative. Skills can be used in professional catering, or to start your own special event business. Heading up a specific subcommittee, such as food or publicity, may fit into your career plan.

Typical Event Committees

♦ Management	♦ Food
♦ Entertainment	♦ Budget
♦ Publicity	♦ Sales and reception
♦ Site	♦ Decorations

Qualifications: A steady temper, a friendly attitude, and at least some creative urges are a good start for this position.

Career Path: In almost every case, an event manager has been in charge of one or more event subcommittees. You can also apprentice yourself directly to an experienced event manager.

Schedule: This can be one of the most time-consuming volunteer positions. Many volunteers report working 5 hours or less each month in the planning stages, but putting in 15-20 hours per week in the last few months before the event. Don't take this position if the event's intense period coincides with a busy personal schedule.

Event Manager (Résumé Items)

- ♦ Calculated and implemented budgets.
- ♦ Selected and confirmed sites.
- ♦ Negotiated with caterers.
- ♦ Publicized to media and organization members.
- ♦ Evaluated results and wrote reports.

Librarian

Although most public libraries demand an advanced degree from their librarians, private corporate libraries often consider business-oriented applicants with volunteer library experience. Generally, the smaller the nonprofit organization, the more room for you to suggest innovations and expansions.

Minimum Library Materials

 ♦ Local, regional, and national newsletters.
 ♦ Relevant books, catalogs, and pamphlets.
 ♦ Copies of local publicity, scrapbook, and photos.
 ♦ Membership list, organization publications.

Qualifications: A knack for organizing is essential. Personal storage space may be expected in smaller organizations.

Career Path: Since this is not a showy position, moving directly to vice president or chapter president is uncommon. However, lateral moves to and from newsletter editor or secretary are easy.

Schedule: This is one of the most flexible positions, in terms of schedule. Almost every task can be accomplished on your own timetable, in your own home. Depending on the volume of materials, you can expect to spend about 7 hours per month.

Librarian (Résumé Items)

 ♦ Ordered, scanned, and cataloged all publications.
 ♦ Organized relevant media clippings.
 ♦ Monitored circulation of library materials.
 ♦ Researched and answered member inquiries.
 ♦ Preserved records/history (files, papers).

Membership Administrator

This position is very good for getting to know new people. If you're shy and trying to overcome it, being membership administrator gives you plenty of opportunity for conversation (and built-in topics).

A Great Greeting Grab Bag

- Welcoming message, membership card, newsletter.
- Calendar of events and programs for current year.
- List of officers and contact information.
- Bumper sticker, poster, pen.

Qualifications: Since you are a representative for the organization, enthusiasm and experience are important.

Career Path: This job is a good alternative for secretaries who find the paperwork dull. If you enjoy the people contact, try becoming a community liaison, program director, or vice president.

Schedule: You may handle incoming calls and send out information packets on an irregular basis. You are usually expected to attend most special events and meetings. If you take on special projects, you give more than 10 hours per month.

Membership Administrator (Résumé Items)

- Created and supervised orientation programs.
- Planned programming for new member recruitment.
- Managed membership database.
- Personally greeted and guided new members.
- Answered questions from members.

Newsletter Editor

If you are just starting out as a freelance writer or artist, contributing to your club's publications gains you valuable experience and portfolio samples. Don't forget to keep your copyright. (See Chapter 9, *For Members Only*.)

Qualifications: Being able to prioritize and meet deadlines is *so* important — you won't improve on the job!

Career Path: Membership administrators, librarians, and secretaries may become interested in this position. It's best to try writing some sample columns or articles before signing on for all the responsibility.

Schedule: Depending on the newsletter's content, you might spend only a few hours retyping and photocopying other people's columns for a quarterly one-sheet letter. On the other hand, you might do in-depth reporting of controversial issues, interview members, read and review relevant books — and spend more than 5 hours per week producing a monthly 4-page newsletter.

Newsletter Editor (Résumé Items)

- ♦ Assigned and edited articles.
- ♦ Arranged for interviews and photographs.
- ♦ Researched and wrote articles.
- ♦ Solicited advertisers.
- ♦ Designed newsletter.
- ♦ Coordinated with printers and post office.

Office Assistant

You can use this position to get your foot in the door at a non-profit organization, or to refresh your clerical skills and re-enter the job market. Unless you're primarily interested in working with a specific set of people, you'll probably leave this job after a year or two.

Qualifications: For some organizations, typing ability, computer experience, or familiarity with office machinery will be required. Other organizations ask only for someone who isn't easily bored by repetitive tasks.

Career Path: An easy promotion to secretary or sales clerk is common. You might choose to specialize as a clerical worker on the treasurer's staff or as a member of the registration crew for special events.

Schedule: If you are assigned to a specific event or program, your hours will increase as the project nears completion. Otherwise, you will negotiate a fixed schedule, between one morning (4 hours per week) and several weekdays (20 or more hours per week).

Office Assistant (Résumé Items)

- Typed letters and reports.
- Photocopied and collated documents.
- Prepared and mailed materials.
- Filed papers.
- Delivered important documents.

Program Director

A flair for showmanship — or prior teaching experience — can pull you into program directing. This position can be a good platform for influencing the philosophy and policies of your organization.

Qualifications: You need to know enough about the subject to evaluate potential speakers. And you may end up playing emcee or substituting for an absent performer, so shyness is a real drawback.

Career Path: Starting as a sales clerk can provide a good background. If you really enjoy the teaching aspect, you might switch to lecturing, or to representing your organization to nonmembers (community liaison or membership administrator).

Schedule: For a full year of monthly seminars, expect to work 10 to 15 hours each month. As a subcommittee chair for a special event, your duties will peak at 8 to 12 hours during the final month.

Program Director (Résumé Items)

- Researched and developed event themes.
- Auditioned, scheduled, and rehearsed performers.
- Negotiated contracts with sites and speakers.
- Selected and reserved meeting places.
- Arranged transportation, lodging, and meals for performers.

Publicist

Membership administrators and publicists both do a lot of public relations. A publicist deals mainly with external media, so it can be a side door into television or newspaper work.

Principles of Printed Pieces

+ No handwritten materials — use typewriter, rub-on lettering, or computer printer.
+ Work in black and white.
+ KISS — Keep It Simple, Sweetheart.
+ Proofread twice, then once more for luck.

Qualifications: Of course, some writing and design ability is a good start for this position, although you can learn on the job.

Career Path: The jobs of newsletter editor and publicist frequently overlap. If you have a lot of people contact, you might move on to community liaison or program director.

Schedule: Like event managers and membership administrators, your job centers around specific projects. Building up to major benefits or recruiting drives, you may spend 15 hours or more a month. During less busy periods, you may work on a new brochure, requiring only a few hours per month.

Publicist (Résumé Items)

+ Proposed and created publicity campaigns.
+ Wrote and designed brochures and press releases.
+ Consulted with artists and printers.
+ Publicized special events, programs, and membership.
+ Acted as spokesperson to media.

Representative/Community Liaison

There are two kinds of representatives: You may represent an interest group within the organization to other areas of the organization, or you may represent the organization to outside agencies (community, state, federal, etc.). External representatives can network aggressively to gain recognition from important members of the business community, especially in politically active organizations.

Qualifications: You can succeed in this position if you balance a strong belief in your organization with a rational assessment of its impact on its members and the community at large. Being able to interact with a diverse group is also a plus.

Career Path: This position is a natural step forward for membership administrators. Its public nature makes a transition to vice president, chapter president, or board member simple.

Schedule: You attend meetings, both in your organization and outside groups. Keeping attuned to community concerns, researching, and calling around also take some time. Expect to contribute about 10 to 12 hours per month.

Representative (Résumé Items)

- Chaired meetings of interest group.
- Attended and reported on meetings of larger group.
- Researched and wrote position papers and articles.
- Received legal documents on behalf of organization.
- Communicated, acted as liaison between groups.

Sales Clerk

You can sell group tours, season memberships, or individual tickets over the phone. Perhaps selling food, books, or art reproductions in a museum store appeals more to you. Getting a closer look at marketing and sales can be invaluable for a potential small business owner. Set sales goals on a regular basis if you want to use this job to get a paid position in a retail store or telemarketing company.

Qualifications: Being able to do sums in your head is helpful. Don't volunteer for the "hard sell" or "cold call" sections if you have no prior experience.

Career Path: This is another beginning position. As soon as you are familiar with the merchandise, you can start. After you gain experience, you can choose to be a treasurer or publicist.

Schedule: Although selling tickets may vary by season, you work a fixed timetable (probably nights and Saturdays). You may schedule 4 hours a month (once a month for a morning) or almost 30 hours a month (a full day every weekend).

Sales Clerk (Résumé Items)

♦ Operated cash register.
♦ Stocked shelves.
♦ Ordered inventory.
♦ Created merchandise displays.
♦ Demonstrated items.

Secretary (Committee)

If you want to brush up on your office procedures before re-entering the job market, this is a step in the right direction. The highly structured, clerical tasks can be boring, but many can be performed at home on your own schedule.

Even in small meetings, make sure that each member is introduced. At large meetings, ask people to stand and say their names when called to speak. Not only does this technique make note-taking easier, but it also encourages socializing after the meeting.

Qualifications: The standard good-attention-to-detail personality works well here. *Don't* take this job if you make a habit of coming late to meetings.

Career Path: Since you would be privy to information on organizational decisions, this could be a path to vice president or chapter president. Sometimes a lateral move to or from librarian or newsletter editor is a natural step.

Schedule: Your tasks are usually centered around a monthly meeting. Before the meetings, you develop and distribute agendas. During the meeting, you take notes. Afterwards, you print and distribute the meeting minutes. This position can be a steady 5 hours a month.

Secretary (Résumé Items)

♦ Reserved meeting rooms and equipment, ordered refreshments.

♦ Distributed official agenda.

♦ Recorded notes for all meetings.

♦ Counted and announced official votes.

♦ Monitored attendance for all officers.

Treasurer

The larger the organization, the more responsibility you will be assigned in this position. The financial tasks can range from simple bookkeeping and ticket-selling to shaping financial policy and investment portfolios. Fund-raising and inventory are sometimes under the umbrella of this office.

If you are thinking of starting a small business someday, being treasurer of a small nonprofit organization is good training.

Qualifications: Being able to balance your own checkbook — and wanting to — are crucial to this job.

Career Path: Professional accounting or clerical experience may make you a logical candidate for treasurer, or you might become interested while working on a fund-raising campaign or event. You might move up to a vice presidency, or step down to concentrate on financial management of one event or department.

Schedule: Most treasurers work longer hours at tax time and at the end of the organization's fiscal year. Unless the budget is excessively complicated, most months you spend 2 hours or less. If you process membership or event checks, add another 5 hours per month.

Treasurer (Résumé Items)

♦ Processed accounts receivable (collected and recorded funds).

♦ Processed accounts payable (calculated, typed, mailed bills).

♦ Prepared and filed tax forms.

♦ Compared and recommended fiscal policies.

♦ Researched and purchased equipment and supplies.

Vice President

The vice president replaces the chapter president in any and all functions when required. Take this apprentice position if you want to move up to chapter president. If you are one of several vice presidents, each vice president carves out a specific niche to oversee (paperwork and chairing meetings, programming and fund-raising, membership and communication, etc.).

Qualifications: Flexibility and a willingness to be second-in-command (at least for a while) are important prerequisites for this office.

Career Path: Being a local officer or working on a special project or committee can lead to a vice presidency. Many volunteers view this position as a sure shot to the chapter presidency; make your ambitions clear when you accept the position. Or, as a former board member, you might welcome the chance to step down and get more involved in a special project as a vice president.

Schedule: You attend meetings, probably once a month for 2 to 3 hours. If you take on special projects, you spend about 10 hours per month on the average. (Note: if your task is a special event or conference, you spend 15-20 hours per week in the last few weeks before the event.)

Vice President (Résumé Items)

- Chaired meetings.
- Monitored issues.
- Researched and wrote reports on disputes.
- Recommended and implemented policy changes.
- Directed programming, recruiting, or budget activities.
- Attended events, practices, meetings.
- Maintained good contact with members.

Volunteer Coordinator

This is one of the fastest ways for you to get experience supervising people. Volunteer coordinators can practice hiring, placing, supervising, and firing workers. During job interviews, emphasize that motivating unpaid volunteers is usually more difficult than motivating paid employees.

Qualifications: Good communication skills are key. The ability to negotiate between staff and volunteers is tested in this job.

Career Path: Membership administrator and event manager are both sister positions.

Schedule: Expect a varied schedule, since you might have a rush of applications from a special event or other publicity. If most personnel turnover happens at a specific time (e.g., end of semester for students), expect a busy season and plan accordingly. Unless you take on special projects, you will average 2 or 3 hours each week at this position.

Volunteer Coordinator (Résumé Items)

♦ Researched and developed job descriptions.

♦ Trained new volunteers.

♦ Organized, supervised volunteers and assignments.

♦ Monitored attendance and hours.

♦ Evaluated performance of individual volunteers.

Part Three

Savvy Networking: People and Politics

Chapter 5

Relationships: It's Who You Know That Counts

"Life is one big *network*," to a top female executive in Washington, DC. She is blunt about her reason for holding one of her board memberships: "The people that I wanted to associate with were on that board and the best way for me to meet them was to be a part of that board. That was how I got an entree into the community. I didn't have children to get me into the school system, I had limited business entree, so I knew the volunteer group could get me into place." (See Graphic 5.1, *Meeting Your Peers.*)

Whom Will You Meet?

You can get to know a variety of people in your nonprofit organization. In fact, some volunteers believe that the same stock characters crop up in every volunteer group. (See Graphic 5.2, *The Bestiary of Volunteer Types, A–Z.*)

Suppose you chair a committee that organizes vendors for the town fair. As a small businessperson, you can establish good relations with local politicians and town workers. You can meet other small business owners, and soon you and your colleagues can exchange secrets of success. You might discover potential suppliers or customers. Members of the same committee can become friends — or even romantic interests.

You may work closely with paid staff of an organization. Be careful: negative attitudes and power struggles are common. A report by the National Research Council revealed that one of the obstacles inhibiting the use of volunteers in schools was "hostility by local teacher and teacher aide organizations."

If you are volunteering in a social service organization, you may also interact with the clients. However, as one staff member who works in a homeless shelter noted, "I think sometimes people are afraid to get involved. Homelessness scares people, addiction scares people."

If you know you would not be comfortable dealing with disadvantaged clients (for whatever reason), you can't be an effective direct service volunteer. Instead, offer to work at administrative tasks that don't involve close interaction with clients, or reexamine your motivations for joining that organization.

After years of dissension, the Jaycees now admit women, and the Junior League now recruits minority members. However, be alert for *subtle* forms of unfairness. Ironically, many women's groups, including the YWCA, allow only women to hold leadership positions. (See Chapter 12, *The Pitfalls of Volunteering*, for further discussion of discrimination.)

Choosing a Professional Association

Since your purpose in joining a trade association is to further business knowledge and relationships, make sure the members are the right people for you.

As a meeting manager, for example, you have several options: Meeting Planners International, the Society of Corporate Meeting Planners, the Religious Conference Management Association, the International Special Events Society, or any of the other meeting planner associations.

During her junior year at college, advertising major Sheryl Fitzgibbon joined the Business and Professional Advertising Association. "I threw myself into it and became newsletter director and program director. The program director is responsible for setting up all the meetings, including choosing speakers. So I was interacting with community businesspeople in my professional field. It was a good way to network, to find out where I wanted to do my internship, and who these people were."

Graphic 5.1 ♦ Meeting Your Peers

Ask an Association

+ Are there many active members in my area?
+ Who teaches your seminars?
+ Are suppliers invited to join?
+ How much experience do most members have in the industry?
+ What are the certification standards, if any?
+ Do most members also belong to another association? If so, which one and why?

And Virginia McCullough finds that her union membership has led to paying jobs. Specifically, "In many ways, the National Writer's Union has helped me in my independent writing business. Using the networking arrangement, I made an important contact for some public relations work with a company through somebody in the NWU."

Getting to Know You

"For the past 20 years, it has been my social life," admits a volunteer who has primarily volunteered for museums and other cultural organizations in Northern California. "I go to fund-raising events, and I enjoy doing that. This is a pretty small community, so you see a lot of the same people at these events. I've gotten to know a lot of people that way, and they're just great people. Pretty soon they become your friends."

Shy volunteers bless the easy friendships formed within non-profit organizations. Since regular meetings and activities are scheduled for you, you can see people casually and frequently. If you wish to expand the friendship, you can suggest activities outside the organization.

You may find, however, that certain relationships wither without the common interest. (This is one of the biggest hazards when leaving an organization.)

A *Autocrats* make everyone do it their way.

B *Bagpipes* drone on (and on) at meetings.

C *Catalysts* help things happen.

D *Dabblers* only do small, short-term jobs.

E *Elastics* bounce back, no matter what.

F *Fountains* bubble over with ideas.

G *Gladhanders* are too busy networking to work.

H *Hunters* are only interested in dating opportunities.

 I *Inquisitors* want to blame anyone but themselves.

J *Jurors* evaluate proposals carefully.

K *Knights* are always rescuing someone.

L *Levitators* rise above petty problems.

M *Motivators* can persuade anyone to do anything.

N *Nesters* settle in one office — for life.

O *Ostriches* ignore problems.

P *Plodders* stick with a project until it's done.

Q *Quilters* put the pieces together.

R *Rebels* always want to try something new.

S *Satellites* hover around "important" people.

T *Trumpets* are always blowing their own horns.

U *Unfaithfuls* never finish projects.

V *Vampires* suck up credit for other people's work.

W *Wallets* throw money at problems.

X *X-rays* know all the gossip.

Y *Yo-yos* can't make up their minds.

Z *Zealots* insist you share their convictions.

Graphic 5.2 ♦ The Bestiary of Volunteer Types, A–Z

Working on a Committee

Your first chance to be a committee chair is exciting, but don't get carried away. If you become chair for a committee with permanent members already in place, get to know people slowly.

Above all, don't just dismiss committee members and replace them with your friends.

Hints for Happy Meetings

♦ *Plan*. Set an agenda and stick to it.

♦ *Ask*. Read up on issues and ask questions.

♦ *Review*. Understand and summarize points of view.

♦ *Schedule*. Start and finish on time.

When you are in charge of forming a committee with the purpose of discussing a single issue or project, it should contain many points of view, or your final consensus is worthless. This means accepting or inviting members with whom you disagree.

You may be surprised to find that your dislike for some people decreases once you work with them. "As volunteers, the committee is all in it together. You're a team," notes Marion Denby, a former volunteer event manager in Washington, DC. (See Graphic 5.3, *Teamwork Puts It All Together*.)

To paraphrase a "For Better or For Worse" cartoon: "I don't know why you're so worried. There are nine people on your committee." "I know, but only three of us *work*." What do you do when committee members aren't pulling their weight? As one volunteer worker pointed out, "The biggest danger of having a chairperson in a small group is that one person ends up taking on all the responsibility. We always burn out our chairperson." Don't let this happen to you. As chair, part of your task is to encourage all to do their share — and to replace them if they don't.

Mentoring: Someone to Watch over You

Among all the different kinds of relationships you develop in a nonprofit organization, a mentoring relationship has the most potential for changing your life.

Graphic 5.3 ♦ **Teamwork Puts It All Together**

Jeanie Austin acknowledges her debt to a more experienced volunteer. "I started out in politics as a volunteer. I was a block captain, and I thought that was the neatest job in the world. Then, my precinct committeewoman retired. She said 'I know the perfect person to become the new precinct committeewoman.' And so I did. It sort of mushroomed after that." In 1989, Austin was elected co-chairman (a paid position) of the Republican National Committee.

Pauline Kezer, speaking at Harvard University on the importance of volunteers in the 90s, commented, "People who volunteer are being recognized as valuable, and being utilized as positive role models for others." Just as you hope that someone notices your efforts and helps you get ahead in the organization, you should fulfill your responsibility to act as mentor for others. "To be really effective, you must *plan* for a transition of leadership," concludes one overworked volunteer. "Someone should be trained and waiting in the wings to be president."

Advice for the New Kid in the Club

If you are a new member, act like a new employee sounding out the corporate culture. For example, don't cling to the only member you know — meet and listen to some other points of view.

"Research has shown that it is best to get new people actively involved within the first three months of joining any type of membership organization. The major reason is that people are eager to find a place to belong and feel accepted, and will search until they find it, especially when they are new to a community," reports Marlene Wilson in *You Can Make a Difference*. (See *Resources*.)

Don't yield to the temptation to sign up for several committees, go to all the meetings, and plunge in enthusiastically. This sort of start is particularly prevalent in hobby and social groups, but *not* recommended. Better to begin slowly, and expand your responsibilities after you've learned the ropes. Otherwise, you'll end up frustrated and overworked — and you may quit as wholeheartedly as you joined.

You must leave room for growth and change in your personal situation and in your relationship with the organization. An officer in student government at San Jose State University, Michael

January 20, 1992

Dear Tom,

Just a note to let you know how much I appreciated your hard work for the New Year, New Notes concert.

When I woke up Saturday and saw all that snow, I thought we were doomed. It was such a relief to find that you had gotten to the church early and cleared the walkways, steps, and driveway.

I gather that you missed everything but the program finale, because you stayed out in the cold, directing traffic and parking cars. (Don't worry — enclosed is a cassette tape of the whole performance.)

Again, thank you for going above and beyond as a member of our congregation.

Gratefully,

Carol Sanderson

Graphic 5.4 ♦ Thank-you Letter

Potter believes in taking things slowly: "At first, I like to just blend in. I survey the scene to see how things work. Then, if appropriate, I like to take a leadership role."

Mind Your Manners

No one minds if a new member of a trade association brings résumés and business cards to meetings; but getting drunk or overly casual at the annual banquet does not win you any points for behavior. At professional and trade association gatherings, mode of dress and conversational taboos are implicit.

A Typical Problem

Perhaps you joined a new club a year ago, and you don't seem to be making friends. Groups where the "personal is political" and where certain people dominate the issues and business of the organization are usually unhealthy. Friendships and cliques are rife, sometimes to a dangerous extent. These are groups where few people make the effort to talk to new members, where no matter how hard you try you are never accepted, and where awards and recognition seem to be delivered by an inner circle — to itself.

Avoid these groups if at all possible, or keep contacts impersonal (read the newsletter, don't attend meetings).

On the Home Front

If your family doesn't share in your volunteer interests, they may resent your involvement. Although most volunteers think that their families are proud of their volunteer work, some encounter problems. As one overcommitted volunteer admitted, "To be candid, my wife says I take too much time away from my family with these outside activities. And I think she's right."

Sometimes it's just a matter of scheduling, as Lelia Fykes-Ridley knows. She is retired and volunteers for a number of organizations. "My husband does not volunteer, because he is still employed. He has no problem with my volunteering, because he is away from the home during that time. I don't think he would enjoy it if it were during his home time. I'm going to be volunteering Wednesday night, but that won't be a problem, because it's only 3 or 4 hours — and it's after his dinner."

Thanks

Gracious letters of thanks sent to staff, vendors, and other members of the business community not only improve your organization's image, but also keep your name and accomplishments prominent.

Don't forget to write thank-you letters to other volunteers who helped you. Treat these as informal recommendation letters. (See Chapter 3, *Promises, Promises*.)

Always be specific in mentioning contributions: "Your comprehensive research on architects allowed the Building Committee to consider each option intelligently"; "I really felt your comments during the budget meeting were to the point, and summed up the picture neatly"; "Before your quick hands came to our aid, our Grecian temple was just plywood." (See Graphic 5.4, *Thank-you Letter*.)

Chapter 6

Powerful Problems and Petty Politics: Negotiating Solutions

You work for months, helping to organize the southeast regional conference of your alumni association. The finance committee outlines the final budget, and all of the speakers are being given free admission. It occurs to you that you must buy a ticket for the conference, even though you contribute many more hours than the speakers do. Can you change this policy?

You just joined a new tennis club, and you enjoy your games. The vice president of the club wins most of the time, and you think it's because she competes against the inferior teams. The matches are supposed to be random, but you don't trust the vice president or her husband (who happens to be the person who sets up the matches). What do you do?

You're an accountant, and you notice that the treasurer is filling out the organization's tax forms incorrectly. You aren't sure whether the treasurer is doing this on purpose — and stealing funds — or out of ignorance. Do you report this to the Internal Revenue Service (IRS)?

Being a volunteer should be a positive, educational, social, healthy experience. One of the techniques you can learn in a volunteer organization is problem-solving. Many organizations allow their members to debate and decide important issues, and you can directly affect national organizational policy.

However, frequently this freedom also involves responsibility, conflict, and negotiation. Being involved in a messy ongoing dispute in your organization can seem overwhelming. (See Graphic 6.1, *Knotty Problems.*)

The Problem-Solving Process

♦ Research the problem thoroughly.

♦ Listen to all points of view.

♦ Recognize personal differences.

♦ Separate and define elements of problem.

♦ Explore and propose alternative solutions.

♦ Go through channels.

What Is the Real Problem?

Untangling the problem or question into separate factors leads to the best, easiest solution or decision. (See Graphic 6.2, *Untangling the Problem Strands.*)

Suppose Eager Edward proposes that refreshments be served at the board meetings of your local club.

Maybe you object for purely *personal* reasons: Slobby Stewart has disgusting table manners, or Busybody Betsy will be snide if you take a second donut, or wine makes you silly. You might think Edward is obnoxious, or that Lonely Lisa will turn your club business meeting into a social event.

Maybe you object for *ethical* reasons: You think that Edward is really drumming up business for his sister's catering business, or you disapprove of junk food, or you don't believe that the club should be paying for your refreshments.

Taking It Personally

As Judith Martin says in *Miss Manner's Guide for the Turn-of-the-Millenium,* "When everyone is volunteering, you would think that the joint cause would be more important than individual

---

Ten Triggers of Tension

♦ Misunderstandings   ♦ Personality clashes

♦ Inexperience   ♦ Mistakes

♦ Unethical behavior   ♦ Apathy or burnout

♦ Loyalties or factions   ♦ Secret information

♦ Power struggles   ♦ Illegal activity

---

egos. That is, you might think that if you had never done volunteer work. Why otherwise efficient and temperate people, many of them demonstrably capable of running the world, should get long-winded and emotional in their extracurricular activities Miss Manners does not pretend to explain. Perhaps it is exactly because their livelihoods are not involved." (See *Resources*.)

Frequently, clubs are stereotyped as hotbeds of gossip, criticism, and jealousy. Far too often, volunteer members become personally involved in organizational disputes.

When an unpopular member like Eager Edward introduces a controversial cause or program, you associate the proposal with the proponent, thinking (and usually expressing) negative thoughts about both.

To test whether your problem is purely personal or not, picture the chief character as Practical Peter, someone you admire, like, or respect; does your view of the situation change? If so, you are obligated to step down from a position of responsibility for this issue, or abstain from voting — your feelings are interfering with your judgement.

If *your* idea is the target of negative opinions, turn the tables. Ask your opponents if they would view the proposal any differently if it were championed by someone else. If your idea is important enough to you, you might be forced to disassociate yourself to give the project a better chance.

In another version of taking it personally, you might have a vested interest in an organizational decision. There is nothing really wrong with this, but be open about your bias — don't cover up your motives. In the "free ticket" problem that opened this chapter, for example, you feel that a benefit is unfairly distributed

Graphic 6.1 ♦ Knotty Problems

to you and others. Another example: as a nonparent, you may actively object to a portion of your membership fee's being allocated to pay for childcare during meetings.

One Rotten Apple

But maybe the problem is indeed one of personality.

Sadly, "kooks" can join any organization. A truly obnoxious person can make every meeting unpleasant, and an unscrupulous individual can bankrupt an organization. "Loose cannons" can drag an organization into a real mess. And a believable pathological liar can quickly split an organization into warring camps.

"I see a kind of indulgence in nonprofits, putting up with folks who can really make trouble and destroy the group," according to one long-time activist. In these cases, you are almost forced to make an issue out of personality. A history of irresponsibility, for example, is relevant when deciding who is to run a new project or program. Pairing up Reliable Roger with Wild Walter seldom works, unfortunately.

Even the Boy Scouts of America keep an Ineligible Volunteer File at national headquarters, so that volunteers who were asked to leave one group cannot join another in a different locale.

Who Is in Control?

Many volunteers relish the freedom to run things their way. Tyranny or power struggles can be the ugly, unfortunate result. For example, should the board of directors for your community theater be allowed to insist that a popular comedy be produced, even though the director wants to showcase a new serious playwright?

Often, arguments over group decisions are focused on line items in budgets, since funding reflects the organization's direction. A fight over money may boil down to a fight over whose projects are more important.

Who Is in the Know?

Sometimes, a major dispute gets started because of unequal access to information.

Graphic 6.2 ♦ Untangling the Problem Strands

Maybe when Eager Edward made his proposal, it was clear to you that he had already talked to Lonely Lisa and Slobby Stewart, and gotten their "yes" votes. It's especially tricky, because Edward might have casually mentioned his proposal while having dinner with Lisa, and suddenly you accuse him of "keeping everything to a special group of friends." In an all-too-common scenario, volunteers are suspicious, simply because they aren't given an opportunity to see a complete budget breakdown for a project — even though they probably wouldn't examine the figures closely if a complicated chart were freely offered.

Always err on the side of telling too much and urge other officers to do the same; openness is vital in a nonprofit organization.

Know What You're Talking About

Your responsibilities as a volunteer member include being informed on organizational issues, especially if you are expected to vote. Read newsletters and review changes in organizational policy.

Always give the benefit of the doubt when you begin your research, even if you are convinced of evil intentions. Feel your way carefully, asking questions and being sure of the answers before taking action.

Maybe you're not getting the whole story; meet and listen to people from both sides of the disagreement. This may not work, especially if you are convinced of the unworthiness of the proposal or the people supporting the proposal. It will rarely change your mind, but it may lead to a compromise or resolution.

For example, financial transactions are complex; mistakes are easily made, and rules may not make sense. Form 990 (a required tax form for nonprofit organizations) is particularly daunting. In a recent study by Connecticut's Department of Consumer Protection, nearly two-thirds (64.2%) of all 990s tested had one or more errors.

Don't Reinvent the Wheel

Your nonprofit organization is more similar to others than you think. Ask volunteers in other groups if the problem has cropped up in their discussions. If so, how did they solve it?

Break Proposals into Features

Don't shoot down an entire proposal by reflex. Eliminating personalities allows you to recognize the positive merits of a plan. Having sorted out what really bothers you, work on modifying the elements you care about.

Ingredients of Compromise

- ♦ "Grandfather" features for long-term members.
- ♦ Delay implementation of some or all features.
- ♦ Set limited trial period.
- ♦ Test on small subset of group.

If you approve of Edward's refreshment plan, but you don't think the club should be paying, propose that each person bring his or her own food. Or move the meeting to a restaurant, and ask for separate checks. If you object to junk food, try to add some healthy options. If you want to keep the meeting businesslike, set aside the first half-hour for eating and socializing, and leave the rest of the meeting food-free. If you're worried about Edward's caterer sister, insist on three competing bids.

Look for Objective Answers

Sometimes, you need to see the bigger picture.

Suppose you discover that Starstruck Stella, who was in charge of table setup for the fund-raising dinner dance, rearranged the seating chart in order to sit with a local celebrity. Rather than publicizing this minor sin and getting nasty about autograph-chasers, maybe you need to propose a new system for seating arrangements that would preclude such personal changes.

Remember to focus on the *future*, not the past.

Go Through Channels

The first way to try to resolve disputes is to bring the dispute to official attention. Describe the conflict to the local chair or chapter president, in as much factual detail and with as little personal commentary as possible. Write the facts down, if it helps you to stick to the point. In the tennis case cited at the beginning of this chapter, for example, don't include how disgusted you are by the public displays of affection between the vice president and her husband.

If this informal discussion brings no action, make your concerns more official by writing a letter to your chapter president. Remember to ask for a *specific* response; do you want a revocation of membership, an immediate vote on a modification of a proposal, a public apology, a resignation, a financial disclosure, or something else?

At this point, something should happen, even if it's just another meeting with you, the president, and the leader of the opposition. Sometimes, the issue goes to an open forum of members, an issue-specific committee, or a higher level of officers in the organization.

Drastic Problems Call for Drastic Measures

You can choose public disclosure, especially in cases where aspects of the problem have already seen print. After an article on the financial troubles of the Boston branch of the NAACP blamed previous volunteers for poor management, a former officer felt compelled to set the record straight. In a letter to the editor, Robert C. Hayden vigorously defended his actions. "I and the incoming board inherited thousands of dollars of debt incurred during Robinson's tenure. However, during my time as president, the branch did pay its national NAACP assessment, paid rent on the headquarters building, and cleared up hundreds and hundreds of dollars of bills while meeting current expenses." (*Boston Globe*, August 13, 1991.)

If the situation seems hopeless to you, you can leave the organization or resign from the committee. In cases where a specific person seems to be at the root of the problem, you could take a short leave of absence, and hope that the troublemaker leaves during that period. (See Chapter 10, *The Volunteer Track*, for advice on graceful quitting.)

If the problem is with another organization, you may be forced to use indirect tactics. If protests to the organization don't work, lobby its major sources of income. Groups representing widely divergent viewpoints have successfully used the same weapon: pressuring United Ways and corporations to withdraw funding from specific causes.

And, of course, you can sue for a variety of reasons, the most common being negligence and discrimination. For example, in 1991, Lauren Cook filed a federal lawsuit because some national parks refused to let her participate in Civil War reenactments on account of her sex.

Is Anyone Being Harmed?

The final decision on whether or not to reveal irregular (but not illegal) activities should be based on one question: are these actions harmful to individuals or the organization, either now or in the future? If the answer is yes, you should meet with the proper officials inside the organization.

Activities which are clearly illegal must be investigated. The accountant in the financial accounting case at the beginning of this chapter, for example, can contact the Internal Revenue Service (IRS) anonymously to research specific regulations for nonprofit organizations.

Remember, especially as a board member, you could be held liable for illegal activities of the organization.

Maybe the Problem Is Bigger Than You Think

Sometimes an issue is common to all nonprofit organizations, and the solution is changing public policy.

As Connie Satterwhite, a volunteer in Cary, North Carolina, complained, "President Bush wants volunteers — but he does not allow many of us to deduct charitable donations and expenses from our taxes. As a hospice volunteer, I drive more than 1,000 miles a year to help care for terminally ill patients; however, I can't deduct these costs from my income tax because my salary and other expenses are too small to itemize. If Bush really wants to encourage volunteers, let him give us a tax break!" (*Newsweek*, July 31, 1989.)

Keep an eye on legislation affecting volunteers and nonprofit organizations. (See Chapter 9, *For Members Only*, for names of periodicals covering nonprofit issues.) For problems like this, coordinate with other groups and petition.

Take Me to Your Leaders

If an issue is important enough to you, act as you would on any consumer problem. Keep trying, and work your way through the ranks of organization officials to argue your case.

Six Ways to Influence Policy

◆ Chair or sit on a committee.

◆ Research aspects of an issue.

◆ Write articles and reports for publication.

◆ Speak informally with other members.

◆ Contribute money for a designated purpose.

◆ Vote formally as a member.

Running for office also provides a good platform for spreading your views. At minimum, you can start debates on issues that concern you. You may lose the election and still win your point. One chair reports, "Another person wanted to be chair, but he wasn't picked. So he didn't take a very active role in the task force. He was absent sometimes, had a bad attitude." This reaction is common when someone loses an election. If you were excited enough to run for office or propose projects and you claimed that you had a lot to contribute, did you lose that energy and commitment when you lost the vote?

Whom Do You Represent?

As the president-elect of the American Dental Association, James Saddoris realized the inherent conflict in an elected position. "I have strong ideas about where I want to lead my association during my presidential term, and I am determined to achieve my goals. But I am still accountable. I am accountable, not to one person, but to 140,000 people. I am accountable to my fellow members of the board of trustees. And so, even while I lead the organization, there will be times when I need to be flexible — times when, as a leader, I will make a deliberate decision to follow the direction of the constituencies to whom I am accountable."

Common Concerns

♦ Who will be affected?
(Explain for each constituency.)

♦ What will happen?
(Give a detailed plan of action.)

♦ When will this action happen?
(Provide a complete schedule.)

♦ Where?
(Research environmental impact.)

♦ Why do it this way?
(List problem and alternative solutions.)

Always remember to ask the opinion of your constituents. You are entitled to wage mighty battles to change that opinion — and expected to provide information on *both* sides of the issue — but you are bound, in the end, to represent the wishes of the people who elected you.

Part Four

What Do You Give, What Do You Get?

Chapter 7

Money:
How Much Bang
for Your Buck?

In 1989, the average yearly contribution of volunteers was $1,022, according to a Gallup poll.

"It's a very hard decision — where to give your money," says a volunteer with a strong social conscience. If you live in California, for example, you are a target for the solicitations of more than 77,000 charitable organizations registered in the state.

Maybe you agree with the Independent Sector, and you "give five [percent of your income] to the causes you believe in."

Perhaps you want to follow the example of many church members, who donate a set portion of their income. Many synagogues ask their members to donate 1.5% of their income. "Tithing is a goal of mine. I'd like to be in a position to tithe 10% — and not necessarily to a spiritual organization," says one volunteer.

Or you may say, like one student, "I don't have very much money. If I see a cause or project that I think is important, I give my time. At this point in my life, that is all I can give."

You contribute money because you are interested in the organization and its goals. And being involved in the financial decision-making ensures that your money goes to support what you believe important. Once you determine how much you want to budget for charitable contributions, review your monetary contributions. (See Chapter 1, *The Right Thing to Do?*)

Do your ideals match the reality? Is your money "doing good?"

Could it be doing better?

From a simple donation, to payment for a Zoological Society of Florida bumper sticker, to United Way payroll deduction, to American Express "affinity" credit cards, the options for contributing become more and more complex.

Before You Contribute

First, find out if the organization meets the standards of the Philanthropic Advisory Service (PAS) of the Council of Better Business Bureaus and the National Charities Information Bureau (NCIB). (See *Resources*.) Unethical organizations may use sound-alike names or addresses, so be careful.

Check Your Charity

◆ Reasonable fund-raising costs.

◆ Active and responsible board of directors.

◆ Ethical fund-raising tactics.

◆ Reasonable administrative costs.

◆ Public accountability.

And always pay by check. (Don't bother with pledges; it costs the organization more to collect and process a pledge than a check.)

For any monetary contributions, you are owed:

◆ Prompt, legal receipt.

◆ Identification of where the money goes.

◆ Clear explanation of applicable tax laws.

Ask and Ask Again

You will be regularly solicited after your first contribution is recorded. Researchers discovered that, once you make your first monetary contribution, it's easier to persuade you to keep giving. Many fund-raisers use last year's patron list as a starting point for this year's appeal; some purchase names of donors to similar organizations and send begging mail. (See Chapter 8, *Volunteer Value*.)

A Business Expense

A survey by the Institute for Nonprofit Organization Management investigated why small business owners make charitable contributions. (Multiple answers were allowed.) The responses: 96% gave "to get involved in the community." But 53% gave because they "made previous donation."

Just as you evaluate your personal donations each year, evaluate your small business donations to be sure that the organizations and kind of donation are in line with your expectations.

Increase Your Contribution — for Free

Want to double or triple your contributions? Ask your employer if the organizations you donate to are eligible for matching gift funds.

Exxon, for example, matches three-to-one. So if you are an Exxon employee and donate $25 to your *alma mater*, it receives $100 total — and it costs you nothing extra but a few minutes to fill out and sign the form. Rice University in Houston, Texas, received more than $1 million dollars in matching gifts by employers of alumni during the 1989–1990 academic year.

A "challenge grant" may be a one-time opportunity, from your employer or other sources, to increase donations. In 1989, the Boston Foundation offered a 50% match for every $1 increase in contributions from designated donors to the United Way of Massachusetts Bay.

Sometimes the matching program requires more than just your money. For example, at Virginia Power and North Carolina Power, the company matches two-for-one donations by qualified employees. You qualify with a minimum of 50 hours of volunteer service per year at an approved organization.

Who Gets How Much?

Have you ever bought lightbulbs, candy, or other products sold door-to-door for a nonprofit organization? Did you ask how much of each dollar was paid to the manufacturer, how much was sent to the national organization, how much remained for the local branch? How much of the profit is a result of the free labor? If the salespeople were paid, were they on commission? How about other for-profit services, such as 900 phone numbers?

Even second-hand shops that look like parts of nonprofit organizations may be privately owned — and skimming a hefty chunk of profit off the top. And used goods donated directly to a nonprofit organization may end up being sold by the organization to for-profit dealers for eventual resale. (See Chapter 11, *Profitable Philanthropy*, for a further discussion of commercialized nonprofits.)

Before you purchase or donate, ask who gets how much.

A Sampling of Nonprofit Products

♦ Aprons (Kiwanis International)
♦ Books (American Management Association)
♦ Buttons (Friends of Animals)
♦ Calendars (Sierra Club)
♦ Cassette tapes (Unitarian Universalist Association)
♦ Coloring books (Xerxes Society)
♦ Duffel bags (Defenders of Wildlife)
♦ Food (Girl Scouts of the USA)
♦ Greeting cards (National Rifle Association)
♦ Jewelry (United States Jaycees)
♦ Maps (National Geographic Society)
♦ Mugs (New England Drama Festival)
♦ Neckties (Harvard University)
♦ Posters (San Diego Symphony)
♦ Soap (Cultural Survival)
♦ Software (American Mathematical Society)
♦ T-shirts (Food First)
♦ Videotapes (The Cousteau Society)

On the Town or on the Streets?

Are disadvantaged people being used to promote and support parties for the affluent?

"I'm not happy with certain kinds of fund-raisers," says one long-time volunteer fund-raiser. "Suppose you buy a $150 ticket: $100 goes for the event, only $50 goes to the charity. I think people are aware it really has a social purpose, as well as a giving purpose. It's a problem that I haven't come to terms with yet."

"Each organization has to develop its own philosophy," as far as Dave Schwartz is concerned. He works with CityTeam Ministries in California. "But be clear to the people you contact, and allow them to decide. If you organize one of those $200-per-plate dinners, tell them how much is defraying the costs and how much is really going back into the organization. Honesty is very important when dealing with donors."

Giving in Circles

Who are the recipients of your money? "Churchgoers may give a larger percentage of their incomes to charities, but much of this is to the church they attend," argues John Morris of Salem, Massachusetts. "The money many churches collect is used mainly to support the church and church employees. This benefits only those who attend the church, the same people who gave the money. The suburban Protestant church I attended while growing up gave, at most, 10 percent of its collections to outreach programs. Simple math tells me that non-churchgoers may, in fact, be more effective in helping truly needy people." (*Boston Globe*, November 12, 1990.)

Surprise: You Support Organizations You Don't Like

You also contribute *indirectly* to many nonprofit organizations.

"Because charitable contributions are deductible from personal income, the government in effect forfeits (under today's tax law) twenty-eight cents of revenue for every seventy-two cents contributed by the wealthiest among us to the charity of his or her choice. This twenty-eight cents is of course paid by other taxpayers — who thus, in effect, make an involuntary contribution to precisely the same charity." (*The New Republic*, May 21, 1990.)

Since corporations who contribute to nonprofit organizations enjoy similar tax breaks, you contribute indirectly in this fashion, as well. (See Chapter 11, *Profitable Philanthropy*.) And nonprofit organizations are generally exempt from real estate tax, sales tax, and taxes on profits.

In *The Nonprofit Economy*, Burton Weisbrod argues that "public subsidies ought to reflect public benefits." (See *Resources*.) Perhaps groups that give back primarily to those who contribute shouldn't be given tax-exempt status or access to government grants.

What Does Your Money Do?

In focus groups conducted by the Public Agenda Foundation, "Nearly everyone felt that *most* charities waste a fair amount of money. Even those who contributed to particular charities said those organizations routinely waste money or spend too much on administration. For example, when asked if the charities that respondents give to waste money, nearly everyone said yes, even when referring to very well respected national charities such as the American Heart Association, the American Cancer Society, and national charities that help people with muscular dystrophy, lupus and diabetes, to name just a few."

Portions of each dollar you give, even in all-volunteer organizations, are distributed in unequal amounts. (See Graphic 7.1, *The Flow of Money*.)

Spend Money to Make Money

Have you ever walked into the office of a nonprofit organization and been disturbed by seeing rooms full of posh furniture? Or maybe you get mad every time you read about the salary of the executive directors of large nonprofit organizations.

As one volunteer, who helps nonprofit organizations with public relations problems, explains, "One of the organizations I'm creating a brochure for operates out of a dumpy building with patched walls. I've been so brainwashed by the 80s! Instead of thinking that their money is being spent on the right stuff, I thought, we need to make this brochure look really good — use slick paper, three colors — in order to show that the organization

Graphic 7.1 ♦ The Flow of Money

is prosperous. It is a dilemma in public relations that bothers me, but when I advise organizations, I end up doing it, too. Because I would not be doing my job well if I said it would be okay to run this off on the office copier."

However, if you really care about the cause, you want the organization to hire the best, most efficient staff possible. In order to do this, the organization must offer *competitive* salaries. If the non-profit sector pays less than the private sector, turnover increases and therefore the organization suffers. Should nonprofit staff be "involuntary donors," forced to give some of their deserved salary to the organization? Since they are not volunteers, they should not be expected to donate time or money.

Control Where Your Money Goes

If you answer a specific appeal, you may be surprised to find out where your money really goes. Organizations can use a flashpoint, such as the nomination of a Supreme Court justice, to raise funds that aren't necessarily directly applied to the cited activity.

The American Red Cross, for example, was thrilled at the generous $53.3 million donated in response to the 1989 San Francisco earthquake. Contributors protested, however, when they learned that the Red Cross planned to spend only $12 million of the total for quake relief efforts and assign the rest to future disasters. Reacting to public outrage and media scrutiny, the policy decision was changed, and all money contributed for quake relief was designated for extraordinary disaster assistance programs in Northern California.

The lesson? Always specify what you expect your contribution to be used for, and complain loudly if funds are redirected.

If you're well-off, creating a small foundation within a larger community foundation (known as donor-advised funds) lets you research organizations, review proposals, and recommend worthy projects — without the complications of creating and maintaining your own private foundation.

Before you contribute through payroll deduction to the United Way, request a list of the organizations and programs that the United Way has deemed worthy of support for that year. Find out the percentage that your local United Way takes off the top; it's probably about 13%.

About 200 United Ways offer donor-choice plans, so you can pick a specific type of organization. Consider sending a separate check directly to the organization of your choice, so that more funds go to the organization, not the United Way. If you prefer payroll deduction for convenience, urge your company to add more options. In Massachusetts, for example, Community Works, a funding agency for 23 social-activist groups, is an alternative that more companies are making available to their employees. And some Massachusetts state employees can choose from more than 600 organizations.

When donating directly, think about restricting your gift to a specific program or part of an organization.

For example, if you donate $5,000 to your *alma mater*, you can earmark all of it for the athletic department. However, you may ultimately be depriving your special interest of funding, because the university may take a corresponding $5,000 out of the department's budget. On the other hand, not every organization behaves that way, and restricting gifts *does* send a message about the importance and/or popularity of a given program. Also, why should only big-gift donors be allowed such control?

Corporate Philanthropy Report noticed a similar rebound phenomenon when Planned Parenthood was dropped from the list of the King County United Way in Seattle, Washington. Local employees, angered by the decision, chose to contribute over $700,000 to Planned Parenthood.

Taxes: What Can You Deduct?

On federal and state income tax returns, you are only allowed to deduct *charitable contributions* if you itemize your deductions. The average deduction for charitable contributions was almost $2,000 in 1989. Taxpayers earning between $25,000 and $30,000 took average charitable deductions of $1,109 that year.

When itemizing, you can generally deduct some portion of your membership fees, so keep copies of cancelled checks and membership cards. When you donate used goods, keep a list of the items and their value. Current prices at resale shops or yard sales can provide guidelines, or read Internal Revenue Service (IRS) publication #561, *Determining the Value of Donated Property*. (See *Resources*.)

Here are some estimated figures for 1992:

♦ Book — $.50 (paperback), $1.00 (hardback)
♦ Coat — $10.00 (adult), $5.00 (child)
♦ Chair — $5.00 (plain), $25.00 (upholstered)
♦ Dress — $5.00
♦ Pot or pan — $5.00 (large), $2.50 (small)
♦ Sofa — $50.00
♦ Suit — $25.00
♦ Sweater — $5.00 (adult), $2.50 (child)

Unreimbursed expenses can sometimes be deducted; keep a travel log and relevant receipts.
You can deduct:

♦ Supplies (stamps, official stationery, etc.)
♦ Transportation (public or private)
♦ Telephone (calls to national officers, etc.)
♦ Uniforms (lab coats, etc., and their cleaning costs)

IRS Publications # 526 (*Charitable Contributions*) and # 1391 (*Deductibility of Payments Made to Charities Conducting Fund-Raising Events*) detail more rules governing tax deductions for volunteer members. (See *Resources*.)

The applicable tax code can be confusing; for example, if you buy a $150 fund-raising banquet ticket, and the *fair market value* of such a banquet would be $50, then you may itemize a contribution of $100 on your tax return.

How do you know what the fair market value is? "Fair market value is the amount the item or benefit would be worth if sold to the general public. *The cost to the charity does not determine fair market value* unless the item was purchased by the charity at the retail fair market value. Donated or discounted goods or volunteer services received in exchange for a payment to charity must be assessed at their fair market value," according to the Independent Sector's booklet, *How Much Really Is Tax Deductible?* (See *Resources*.)

If you take a volunteer vacation and travel to exotic spots to work on volunteer projects, keep a daily work log and don't play tourist on the same trip, or you may not be eligible for full deductions.

Chapter 8

Volunteer Value: How Much Are You Really Worth?

You're part of a billion-dollar business: Volunteer time is worth about *170 billion dollars* per year. According to a Gallup survey, volunteer hours in 1989 totaled 20.5 billion — the equivalent, roughly, of 10 million full-time jobs.

"I can't put any cost on it," says a student volunteer who puts many hours each week into her organization. "If I wanted, I could use all the time I put into my volunteer activities to get a paying job, and make money that way. But that isn't what I want to do. I am achieving my goals and I like what I'm doing as a volunteer."

How much are you *really* worth to your organization?

How Much Do You Donate?

Nonprofit organizations can accept donations of time, money, and a range of other items — and *sell* your donated books, clothes, blood, and services, plus your name and address. (See Graphic 8.1, *How Do You Give?*) You can give or lend money or equipment to your nonprofit organization. If you own your own business, or you're high enough in the corporate structure, you can lend the ultimate resource — people.

Pay Your Dues Promptly

Organizations usually rely on a small budget and work force, and every late-paying member means more time and money spent on bills, reminders, and cancellations. Like shoplifting, this ultimately results in higher prices (dues). Also, in small organizations your dereliction is likely to become common knowledge, and your financial reputation may suffer.

If You Can't Deduct

If, like two-thirds of Americans, you don't itemize on your tax return, then you can't deduct gasoline, postage, telephone calls, or other supplies purchased or used for your nonprofit organization. (See Chapter 7, *Money.*) Therefore, these "contributions to the cause" are an added expense in the grand total of your donations.

Who Pays the Babysitter?

Whether you itemize or not, you can't get a tax deduction for dependent care expenses during volunteer time, so try to get reimbursed for babysitting fees, or propose that the organization provide centralized childcare during meetings and special events.

However, childcare (either reimbursing individuals or hiring group babysitters) is a sticky issue for most nonprofit organizations, because of issues of liability, discipline, and fairness.

Most organizations have not developed a formal policy about children. Urge your group to evaluate the current situation and formulate a long-term policy. Remember that parents and non-parents are usually divided on the question; take both opinions into account, and compromise.

They're Selling Your Name

If you donated to the Davis Memorial Goodwill Industry in the Washington, DC, area, or the Animal Welfare Association of New Jersey, your name and address are being sold to direct-mail marketers. Associate members of the American Museum of Natural History and the Smithsonian can expect more mail, too.

Donors to the Muscular Dystrophy Association should be glad that there are some limits: your name is sold only to nonprofit fund-raisers, and telemarketing is not allowed.

Graphic 8.1 ◆ **How Do You Give? Count the Ways**

Finally, the three major credit-reporting companies sell credit reports to nonprofit organizations.

Selling membership lists to mail-order businesses is a lucrative sideline for many nonprofit organizations. Some groups prohibit this practice in their charter or allow each regional group to decide its own policy. If your group does decide to sell your mailing list, try to retain the right to approve or veto the contents of each mailing a buyer makes.

Some volunteers insert a false middle name to track who is selling names to which organizations, but some people decry this tactic, since it wastes paper and increases fund-raising costs for the nonprofit organizations involved.

It's easier to directly ask each organization to remove your name from such merchandising lists. On items carrying first-class postage, you can write "return to sender" and "delete from list" on the envelope and put the material in the mailbox. Also, write to Mail Preference Service, Direct Marketing Association, 11 West 42nd Street, P.O. Box 3861, New York, NY 10163, to get your name barred from thousands of lists.

Whose Money Is It Really?

As part of volunteer recognition programs, many companies donate money in honor of employees' volunteer efforts, so your Volunteer of the Year award might lead to a very tangible gift to your volunteer organization. Another example of indirect funding: to encourage employees to participate in a walkathon, your employer might offer to contribute a set amount per person, per mile walked. (See Chapter 11, *Profitable Philanthropy*, for a closer look at the economics of these kinds of situations.)

Time Is Money

As a fund-raiser, a ticket-taker, a speaker, a cook, or a pair of helping hands, you give time and effort to benefit the organization. If you didn't do this work, either the organization would be forced to pay someone or the project wouldn't happen. In 1984, almost half of the workforce in the nonprofit sector was volunteers.

Use the professional job description you developed in Part Two, *Join Today, New Job Tomorrow*, to estimate what the salary would be for your volunteer job if it were a paid position. Value your time accordingly. Always ask yourself if your effort is worth the payback for the organization — and for you. (See Chapter 12, *The Pitfalls of Volunteering*.)

Are You Volunteering for a Cause — or a Corporation?

Perhaps your company, like many others, encourages volunteering for specific causes. For example, if a local television station needs volunteer callers for a telethon, your company agrees to provide employees — and your company's logo is prominently displayed behind the phone bank.

When you participate in these arrangements, remember that you are acting as an unpaid member of the public relations staff.

Loaning Money to an Organization

Avoid reimbursement arrangements (you pay for items or services up front, and the organization pays you back later) whenever possible. Unless your organization is very new or very small, the treasury should advance funds to you covering items for special events, publications, etc. Use an organizational charge account at local businesses, if possible.

Quick and Easy Reimbursements

♦ Estimate the costs ahead of time.

♦ Seek prepurchase approval from the treasurer.

♦ Stay within the budget guidelines.

♦ Use the group's tax-exempt number.

♦ Request receipts and keep photocopies.

♦ Submit reimbursement requests immediately.

♦ Cash checks promptly.

Chapter 9

For Members Only: What's in It for You?

"Be clear about what the motivation should be for volunteering. It is not the promise of material reward. I don't want to say that financial sacrifice must be involved, but if it is, it seems to me that makes it even more ennobling," declares Clark Kent Ervin, associate director at the Office of National Service.

Contrast Ervin's view with student Michael Potter's honest appraisal of his volunteer work on political campaigns as "an investment in my future career." However, Potter has another, more emotional reason for getting involved in politics. "If you just believe what you read in the newspapers, you don't know what's really going on. But by getting involved in politics, you really see how things work behind the scenes."

You may be reluctant to assign value to your volunteer participation, but it is part of your evaluation process to examine what tangible — and intangible — benefits are being exchanged. (See Chapter 1, *The Right Thing to Do?*) "I have contributed my services to several organizations since I was a teenager," wrote one volunteer in a letter to an advice columnist. "Some treat me as though they were doing me a favor by letting me work there. Quite a few think a certificate and a tea party adequate compensation for a year of aggravation and frustration."

The widow of film star Danny Kaye, Sylvia Fine Kaye, gave $1 million to Hunter College for restoration of a theater. The tradeoff? The playhouse was named in honor of the couple.

Even if you aren't a celebrity, your name on a petition may result in a change in the laws of your state. You may learn new skills (or meet new people) at your volunteer job that translate into a promotion or career jump. Maybe the money you raised sent a city child to summer camp in the country, or the man you taught to read got a better job. Perhaps you discovered a friend, roommate, business partner, or spouse as a result of your volunteer project.

In return for some of your monetary donations, you may be entitled to tax deductions. Or, instead of a tax deduction, you may receive goods or services (newsletters, light bulbs, buttons, etc.). (See Chapter 7, *Money*.)

What you're really looking for is a win-win situation: one in which the sum of your contributions to the organization is *in balance* with the sum of what you feel the organization gives to you and to those people and causes you care about. Like Lelia Fykes-Ridley, who sells memberships two days a week at a museum in Illinois, your evaluation might show a happy reciprocity. "I felt that I was needed here. I felt very good, and very welcome. I was able to do well at selling. And that was profitable for the museum, but it was also good for my ego." (See Chapter 12, *The Pitfalls of Volunteering*, for further discussion.)

Are There Tangible Benefits?

At a museum, for example, typical tangible membership benefits include:

- Free or discount tickets or admission.
- Invitations to member-only events.
- Free coat-checking or lockers.
- Reserved seating at public events.
- Discounts at museum giftshops and restaurants.
- Publications.

At the University of Chicago Hospitals, senior citizen volunteers are given free lunches, and volunteers are given bus fares, parking passes, jackets, and other items.

As a student, you may take advantage of stipend arrangements that allow you to work as an intern for nonprofit organizations. In return for teaching or other work at low-paying or public jobs, your student loan payments may be deferred or reduced. In professional associations, you are usually eligible to win a scholarship or conference expenses.

Exchanges

You may be promised direct benefits for specific donations. For example, Ogilvy & Mather Direct, an advertising agency in New York, wanted to encourage employees to contribute to the annual United Way campaign. Employees who donated received a day off, and those who donated within a week of being asked were given two days off. A local J.C. Penney store in Salt Lake City, Utah, gave free perfume to March of Dimes' volunteers who turned in their collected donations on a specific day — and free facials to volunteers who raised $35 or more.

As a small business owner, you may exchange your professional services (catering, printing, etc.) for free publicity (a name credit on the program, business cards or brochures on the reception table).

In a booklet called *The Time Dollar*, Edgar S. Cahn explores a straightforward example of exchanging volunteer work on an organized basis. (See *Resources.*) In this service credit system, volunteer hours are "banked" at a one-hour-equals-one-credit rate.

You have many spending options, Cahn explains. "You can use these credits to get help for yourself, or you can save them up until you're in need. You can also donate your credits to a relative or friend or to a general fund that helps people unable to earn credits themselves. Unlike the traditional approach of volunteers, the service credit system recognizes that many people who may need help can also help others, in different ways."

What Money Can't Buy

Rita Webb Smith, a community activist in New York City, was interviewed in the premier issue of *Lear's*. "People say volunteering isn't worth much because you don't get paid. Let me tell you, you get a lot of other things money can't buy."

The chance to put your mark on something is rare. A student who chaired the planning committee for a neighborhood park marvels, "It was only a few hours of my time, but that park is permanent. For the rest of my life, I'm going to be able to visit it and see my ideas at work. I can point to where I had them round a corner; it would have been a square if I hadn't suggested we should curve it."

The feeling of accomplishment you get from your volunteer work can be the biggest benefit. "Sometimes business is off," admits Carl Cookson, chairman of the Santa Clara Land Title Company in San Jose, California. "So sometimes the victories I get are on the outside — fund-raising and helping other community projects."

If you edit a newsletter, for example, read letters from people who enjoyed particular articles, and remind yourself how circulation has grown since you started. Save particularly positive letters or other feedback for your portfolio, and attach copies to your résumé.

And preliminary research seems to indicate that you can get a "helper's high" from your one-on-one volunteer activities. "The Institute for the Advancement of Health, an information clearinghouse in San Francisco, surveyed thirty-three hundred volunteers and found that those who had weekly personal contacts with charity recipients reported less stress in their daily lives and an increased sense of well-being and self-worth." (*Ladies' Home Journal*, December, 1990.)

A Volunteer's Education

"I can't tell you how many educational opportunities I have had as a result of volunteering," says Pauline Kezer, a former state legislator in Connecticut, who credits her career success to her involvement in the voluntary sector.

Take advantage of any training that interests you within the organization.

As a volunteer for the Girl Scouts of the USA, for example, you gain access to a terrific free training program. "Last year, 2,235 adult volunteers completed top-level seminars on service marketing, financial planning, property management, and other topics. Tens of thousands of others, from volunteer troop leaders to the executive directors of councils, also ran through local training programs." (*Business Week*, March 26, 1990.)

Network Shamelessly

"You never know who you're going to meet," is the savvy philosophy of a businesswoman who volunteers with several organizations, including a youth-service group, an alumni club, a theater company, a women's organization, and a business association. Attending meetings and events is a constant education. What is the greatest resource the organization provides? The other members. Meet and talk to everyone; ask questions.

Knowledge at Your Fingertips

This book shows that it is up to you, as a volunteer, to seek out training opportunities. Don't operate in a vacuum! Take advantage of publications designed for volunteer workers.

Start by establishing a lending library for your local organization. There are many useful books on specific subjects of interest to volunteers. (See *Resources*.)

Three Recommended General Publications

♦ *The Chronicle of Philanthropy* (biweekly newspaper)
♦ *The NonProfit Times* (monthly newspaper)
♦ *Nonprofit World* (bimonthly magazine)

Meeting News, Cooking for Profit, and *Successful Meetings* can give good suggestions to event managers. If you work on the program committee, ask your organization to subscribe to *The Toastmaster* or *Campus Activities Programming*. If you're trying to raise money, *Contributions, Fund Raising Management*, and *Grassroots Fundraising Journal* have great ideas. Volunteers in charge of public relations may find guidance in *Channels*. And volunteer treasurers can search through copies of *Free Materials for Schools and Libraries* to find good bargains. Even volunteers with relatively specialized jobs may be able to subscribe to helpful publications such as *Church Media Library Magazine*.

If you're a local officer, check out the national office; it may stock or produce relevant handbooks or magazines (a few examples: *Discovery YMCA, Girl Scout Leader*, and *VFW Auxiliary*).

And free subscriptions to catalogs such as *Volunteer Readership*, *Volunteer Energy Resource Catalog*, and *Volunteer Marketplace* let you find out about the latest books and materials. (See *Resources* for information on all of these publications.)

Make room for these purchases in your group's budget. The information you get will save you and your fellow volunteers time and money.

The Learning Is Easy

"I learned far more about team management, dealing with politics, marketing and sales, and getting along with people in organizations in my volunteer work over the past two years than I've ever gotten in my entire career as a software engineer," says Rich Braun, a Massachusetts volunteer. His experiences included planning a rally attended by 2,000 people.

Want an expert to teach you how to take photographs, design brochures, plan events, write newsletter articles, use computers, make centerpieces? The Council for Advancement and Support of Education (CASE), the American Society of Association Executives (ASAE), and the Support Centers of America teach skills to nonprofit workers all around the nation. (See *Resources*.)

And other organizations offer classes of interest to volunteers. Here are just a few examples. In North Carolina, a volunteer coordinator can learn "How to Work Effectively with Volunteers" at the North Carolina Justice Academy. A newsletter editor in Florida can explore the "Basics of Newsletter Production" in a program sponsored by Volunteer Jacksonville. "Public Relations on a Shoestring" is a course offered by the Los Angeles chapter of the Public Relations Society of America. And a chapter president in Pennsylvania might find out about shaping group dynamics at the "Volunteers: Fact and Fiction" symposium in University Park, Pennsylvania.

Encourage your nonprofit organization to fund your enrollment. Offer to take complete notes and make them available to all, or to pass on what you learn. Alternatively, ask your employer to donate your tuition.

Informal networking with similar organizations can yield great benefits. Or, affiliate with a national umbrella group: a good example is the Friends of Libraries U.S.A. (See *Resources*.)

Try to work at a number of different jobs, to keep both your interest and your learning levels up. Remember: Monitor your work and contributions. Set goals; use time sheets and other feedback to mark your personal development.

Learning Never Ends

Each time you want to be promoted in your organization, ask to be apprenticed to the departing volunteer for a few months, so that you have a chance to learn the ins-and-outs of the job before assuming full responsibility. Once you've mastered a skill, teach a deputy. You'll put the final polish to your expertise, and have a trained person ready to take on your office or project.

What Do You Earn, What Do You Learn?

"Marjorie Meinhardt earned her bachelor's degree in two and a half years, starting when the youngest of her six children entered school. She got academic credit for her experience with Little League fund-raisers and other volunteer activities and for a four-month internship as a nursing home administrator." (*Changing Times*, January 1989.)

If possible, choose training that awards Continuing Education Units (CEUs); these credits can be listed on your résumé and may help you qualify for certification in a profession.

If you're interested in college credit, the Educational Testing Service publishes *How to Get College Credit for What You Have Learned as a Homemaker and Volunteer*. (See *Resources*.)

And a growing number of universities, including Case Western Reserve, Duke, Indiana University, and Yale, offer courses on philanthropy, nonprofit management, and community service. (See *Resources*.)

Michael Levine runs an internship program at his public relations firm in California. Convinced by the success of his own program, Levine is working to promote interning and increase the percentage of college students interning from the current ten percent to fifty percent. Many schools offer independent study classes, which can often be fulfilled with volunteer projects in your field of interest. For some students, theory can become practice with a nonprofit organization — and material for a résumé.

When he researched community service in schools, Dennis Smith, a regional representative for the United States Department of Education, found a number of school systems that gave academic credit for volunteer work, including programs in Georgia, Michigan, Maryland, and Washington, DC. (See Chapter 12, *The Pitfalls of Volunteering*, for more discussion of curriculum reform.)

What's Yours Is Yours

If you create something for your organization, such as a booklet or logo, make sure the copyright is registered in *your* name. If you contribute a recipe to a community cookbook, or write a column for your group's newsletter, make sure that *your* name and a copyright symbol appears on the item itself.

You may wish to grant only one-time rights, so that the organization must ask you before printing another edition. Keep the right, if the organization wants to make changes in your work, to remove either your name or your work if you're unhappy about the changes.

V.I.V. (Very Important Volunteer)

Jeanie Austin of the Republican National Committee related this anecdote to illustrate her feelings about the proper place of volunteers in politics. "I walked into an event in Michigan six months ago. I was being introduced, saying hello to everyone. The organizer took me around, mentioning what each volunteer did. She told me about this young lady who was at one of the tables waiting to make nametags. She said that this woman volunteered many, many hours, and came down to help whenever she could, because she loved politics. I held out my hand and said, 'Hi, I'm Jeanie Austin, I'd like to meet you.' She said, 'I'm not anybody, I'm just a volunteer.'

"And I said, 'You are the most important person in this whole room. Without you, we couldn't be here. *You* are the V.I.V. — Very Important Volunteer.' And I meant it. If you have no volunteers, there is no heart in the campaign."

According to the experts, recognition is a cornerstone of effective volunteer programs. It comes in many forms, including a host of "volunteer recognition" items (bags, balloons, books, buttons, certificates, clocks, earrings, hats, keychains, mugs, paperweights, posters, sweatshirts, ties and tie clips — even Frisbees. Most are imprinted with the organization's logo or an inspirational slogan. (See Graphic 9.1, *Kinds of Awards*.)

If you're in charge of rewarding volunteers (as volunteer co-ordinator or member of the awards committee), write for free catalogs from the NATIONAL Volunteer Center and the Volunteer Services Division of the California Association of Hospitals and Health Systems. (See *Resources*.)

Gestures of Gratitude

♦ Informal "well-done" handshake.

♦ Thank-you letter.

♦ Recommendation letter.

♦ Promotion to higher volunteer position.

♦ Scroll, plaque, or other award item.

♦ Your name in the local newsletter.

♦ Your picture in the local newspaper.

♦ Life membership.

♦ Being the guest of honor at your own awards banquet.

Not Rich, but Famous

Want to get your picture in the paper? Karen Kriley, a United Telephone System's employee in Butler, Pennsylvania, volunteers for several organizations, including the Salvation Army, the March of Dimes, and the Special Olympics. Not only does Kriley get a good feeling about doing good, but also she appeared in three photos in one issue of *Excel*, UTS's corporate magazine.

You could even receive national recognition as a Point of Light. Ines Pegeas was invited to meet with President George Bush in 1990 because of her success with Hartford Areas Rally Together (HART), a local program in Connecticut to rid city neighborhoods of drugs.

Graphic 9.1 ♦ Kinds of Awards

Who Decides?

Kathleen Ann Kaminski was named an "Outstanding Young Woman of America." Nominations came from a friend in New York and a former employer in Ohio, but Kaminski then had to provide references, and list all of her community service projects and organizations.

Maybe no system of awards exists in your organization, or a maze of policies governs even the smallest gesture of gratitude. Every member may be able to nominate any other member, or perhaps a select award committee makes all the decisions, or perhaps awards are voted on by the membership as a whole.

Maybe you recognize the system this volunteer describes: "It's a case of the squeaky wheel gets the grease."

No matter what system is in place, your duty is to try to make sure that deserving members (including yourself) receive appropriate awards.

For example, while you may not be able to formally nominate another member because you aren't a voting member, you could certainly write a letter of recommendation to the committee.

It is tacky to write a letter of recommendation for yourself. However, any letter for someone else would naturally mention your mutual work (committee members, event managers, etc.) — but don't overdo it, or you may be seen as sleazy.

You should always keep your volunteer résumé up to date; if you know that you are being considered for an award, make a copy available to committee members.

Where Do I Put This Brass Plaque?

A volunteer who has collected twenty years' worth of award items used to hang his many awards on the wall in his office, "but then I decided that people would think I was bragging, so I took them down."

You may, however, be one of the many businesspeople who join community groups and professional associations specifically to earn certifications and meet prospective customers. Tokens and prizes from hobby and social groups, however, should probably be left at home.

Speech, Speech

Congratulations! You won the top honor for community service in your town's school system. The banquet is next Saturday. Like Carl Cookson, who won the 1990 Volunteer Fund-Raiser of the Year award from a local branch of the National Society of Fund-Raising Executives (NSFRE), you may be "very nervous about what to say."

Follow his lead: "Of course, I thanked them. I said that I got more out of doing it than whatever funds I raised. I knew the organization had grown in the last couple years, and that growth meant more people raising more money for worthy organizations. I ended by saying that it was really a healthy sign for the future. Then I sat down."

Tips for Thank-you Talks

♦ Practice, practice, practice.

♦ Avoid smugness or self-congratulation.

♦ Don't fake surprise.

♦ Keep it short — under 5 minutes.

The important people to remember in your acceptance speech are your family (if your time contribution was considerable) and then your coworkers. When you volunteer for a social service or political organization, you are expected to discuss how your effort furthers the cause.

If you are notified in advance (or you suspect), prepare and practice a short speech. Remember, that 3-minute acceptance speech may be the first or only time some people meet you. And practice prevents your forgetting colleagues and family in the crunch, and makes you sound polished and professional.

When You Don't Hear Your Name

However, especially in all-volunteer organizations, effort and recognition frequently don't match. As one long-time volunteer noted ruefully, "At first, I would really go all out for a project, try and make a significant contribution — and no one noticed. I would go to the event, and other people would be thanked for their work, but not me. Maybe it's just how I am: I'm not usually out in front, I'm usually working in the background. Still, it bothered me, but what was important was how I felt about what I had done. Then I went into a phase where people began to recognize my work. Now I find that I get credit sometimes when I don't even deserve it. It is out of balance."

And, he acknowledges, "It takes a lot more than one person to make something happen. I have never done anything without a lot of people working on it. It may not sound as grand as claiming all the credit, but my strength has been to put together a lot of people to help."

Not receiving an award that you feel you deserve is very disappointing. And watching someone else receive that award, and believing that he or she is less deserving than you, can sour the most even-tempered volunteer.

Unfortunately, hard work is not always its own reward. Award committees are not perfect; they can make mistakes. And some, especially on the local level, are motivated almost entirely by favoritism. Sometimes, too, a volunteer with a "showy" project or position will garner more attention than a volunteer whose work is performed at home or with people outside the group.

Other than crying — or crying foul — what can you do? You have a range of options, from changing the entire award system in your organization, to quitting the group in protest. (See Chapter 6, *Powerful Problems and Petty Politics*, for advice and techniques.)

Part Five

A Volunteer's Dilemmas: Evaluations and Ethics

Chapter 10

The Volunteer Track: Choosing the Right Path

When his son first became interested in athletics, Michael joined a group that oversees youth sports. He coached for a year, then became a policymaker in the local group. After a few years, he was a regional officer, and organized regional contests. His son leaves for college this fall, and Michael is thinking about resigning his membership.

Always an avid reader, Ellen joined a local literacy group to help adult nonreaders. Starting as a clerk, she worked her way up to head of publicity and supervised other volunteers. She began to be impatient with the "sloppy" methods of other volunteers and the way the group was run. The president and Ellen met last week, and argued. Ellen was told that she had grander ideas than the budget allows.

Alex worked hard for local and state political campaigns. He carried signs, circulated petitions, and contributed faithfully. Last week, the senator's aide asked Alex to organize the upcoming convention caucuses in his precinct.

Debby joined a local women's club to meet new friends. She volunteered eagerly for a variety of tasks and events, and soon she knew everyone's name. Debby just ran for vice president — and lost.

Mark has been a member of a garden club for over a year now. He has sponsored several innovative proposals. The older members, however, seem more interested in backyard flower borders than environmental issues. A small group of younger members have begun to meet regularly at Mark's house.

Once a joiner, always a joiner? I bet you recognized yourself or other volunteers you know in the composite models above. Each is at a turning point in his or her volunteer life. (See Graphic 10.1, *Turning Points on the Volunteer Track.*)

Take a Good Look Around

Stop! Estimate and reconsider your volunteer time and money contributions at regular intervals. The end of the semester is a natural evaluation time for interns, for example. Or total up your time and monetary contributions when your annual renewal form arrives. (See Chapter 1, *The Right Thing to Do?*)

Ask yourself all the choosing and joining questions again. Make sure that the organization is still fulfilling your needs — and that you are still effective in the organization.

Are you getting and giving your best?

Usually, your choice of organizations over the years changes to reflect your lifestyle choices.

If your primary reason for joining a hobby group was social, you might cut down on your involvement after you get married. If a disease or tragedy strikes, you might join a group like Mothers Against Drunk Driving (MADD) or the American Cancer Society (ACS). People who purchase a home often take up community and local political issues. If you become a parent, you find yourself more involved with children's extracurricular activities; perhaps you join a Parent Teachers Association (PTA). As you reach your fifties, you may become a member of the American Association of Retired Persons (AARP).

Burnout

"Volunteering opens doors. Remember, whatever activity you choose, it should be *fun*. If it isn't, try something else," urges a dedicated volunteer who belongs to several organizations.

Do you feel that you are putting more and more time into an organization and getting less and less satisfaction out of it? "It is explained that all relationships require a little give and take," said Quentin Crisp, an English essayist. "This is untrue. Any

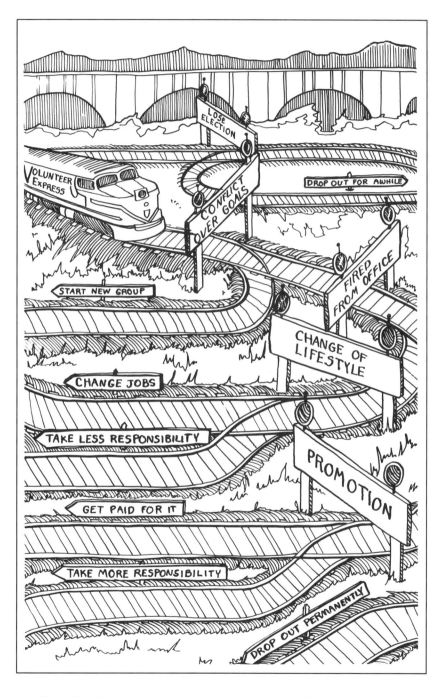

Graphic 10.1 ♦ Turning Points on the Volunteer Track

partnership demands that we give and give and give and at the last, as we flop into our graves exhausted, we are told that we didn't give enough."

Burnout Babble

♦ "I don't care."

♦ "It's no use."

♦ "Not that issue again."

♦ "I've got better things to do."

♦ "Boy, that really irritates me."

♦ "I can't believe we have to . . ."

♦ "Nobody notices how hard I work."

♦ "What a waste of time and money."

♦ "I just can't stand him, that's why."

♦ "I know I said I would, but . . ."

♦ "Nobody appreciates me."

A concerned wife complained to an advice column about the behavior of parents involved in children's team sports. "The negatives . . . have turned off my husband. He is frustrated with adults who break rules, hurt children's feelings, and spend more time with their children than with other players. The politics in the local league are uglier than government elections." If you think the organization (or its members) is at fault, use the techniques in Chapter 6, *Powerful Problems and Petty Politics*, to examine your alternatives.

Something is wrong — but it may be you, not the organization. Focus on your current projects, and differentiate between a long-lasting problem and a passing irritation. Perhaps what's really bothering you is your paid job, or your friends or family. A brief period of inaction can bring perspective in such cases.

If your only social life and connections are in the organization, you are probably too involved. Sometimes people in "12-step" organizations trade their original addiction for an addiction to the 12-step program and its members. Do you spend all your free time with people who belong to the bowling league? Does your social life revolve around your church and its members? Such insular behavior can be detrimental, so consider gearing down your activities, and expanding your circle of friends to include "outsiders."

The "Volunteer Track"

After a year or two with a group, you should be in a good position to move upward in the organization. "We allow our volunteers to find their own niche," said one volunteer coordinator.

Unless you prefer the lower-level tasks, move onward and upward, for two reasons: the group should have experienced members in policymaking jobs, and newer members should have a chance to get involved. In a healthy organization, there should be a steady cycle of newer members joining, gaining experience, being given more responsibility, training their replacements, and being promoted.

Although you may choose at any point to switch into a salaried job, there are natural progressions for volunteers who stay in one organization. One such example is outlined below.

Climbing a Ladder of Volunteer Responsibilities

- Fund-raising committee member (cook for banquet).
- Publicity committee member (address envelopes).
- Fund-raising chair, local (direct events).
- President, local (overall administration).
- Fund-raising officer, regional (direct events).
- Publicity officer, national (spokesperson to media).
- President, national (overall administration).

Narrow Your Focus

As you gain experience, you'll realize which volunteer jobs suit you. Concentrate on the organizations and tasks that really catch — and keep — your interest.

"In this last year, I've decided I can continue contributing, but in a different way," said a volunteer in Northern California. "I'm convinced that there is too small a group working on community projects. So I switched to the nominating committee for the museum, and I'm chairman of the nominating committee for the arts center. Our only task is to see if we can get new people involved."

And don't get stuck in the rut of doing the same thing year after year, just because everyone says you're "so good at it."

It's All Mine

Pat Morgan, development officer at St. Andrew's School in Bethesda, Maryland, speaks from experience: "If it's your project, you started it — it's hard to let go and let someone else do it."

And a board member who pitched in right from the creation of an organization ruefully agrees. "I was so involved in the Children's Discovery Museum that I felt *ownership* as president. When the new president came in, I almost resented him. I had to stop going to meetings for a while, because nothing he could do would be right with me. And he's one of my best friends! It was really an emotional thing. I've seen that happen in other organizations, and I knew it was wrong. This guy is such a good friend that he saw what was going on and brought me back in."

Frequently, you'll find yourself reluctant to say no to an event or committee that you founded, even if you should. According to Dave Schwartz, who supervises volunteer counselors, "If a volunteer establishes a program, you have a volunteer for life. As soon as your volunteer has ownership of a program, you can consider him or her to be a permanent volunteer."

Despite the lure, *never* chair the same committee or repeat the same project for more than two years in a row — don't burn yourself out. Also, you need to let the newer members assume responsibility.

You Can't Fire Me, I'm a Volunteer

Sheryl Fitzgibbon, president of the San Jose State University chapter of the Business and Professional Advertising Association, knows firsthand about firing volunteers. "It's so *hard* to say, 'I'm removing you from your position, because you aren't fulfilling the needs of the office.' I always try to give everyone as many chances as I can — but you know when someone is not working out. Two of our officers had to resign because, in my opinion, they just couldn't put in the time and effort that officers should."

And, Fitzgibbon insists, even volunteers who quit a project can still be members. "They still wanted to be a part of what we were doing: to be friends, to attend our meetings and social events."

Where Do You Go from Here?

"We see people drop in and out of volunteer service all the time," says Patrick Shannon, director of volunteer services at the University of Chicago Hospitals. "Sometimes, people experience changes in their lives, and they need to devote more time to that — romantic involvements, job changes, illness in the family. Sometimes, they just burn out. Among our elderly volunteers, some take the winter off."

Change Your Life

A student volunteer was so energized by his work on election campaigning that he changed his life instead of his volunteer work. "I switched to political science from business marketing. I enjoyed it so much. I had no problem working so many hours, because it was something that I felt really good about."

Change Organizations

You may become so frustrated with an organization that you quit completely and join another organization.

You may be tempted to begin a new group which you hope avoids the problems of the original organization. (This syndrome is why there are so many nonprofit organizations in the United States working on similar projects.)

Think *carefully* before you start an organization. It's counterproductive when organizations in the same category duplicate efforts, or work at cross-purposes. Between 1982 and 1987, over 100,000 new service organizations were created; I'm sure that many of them were unnecessary.

For example, cause-of-the-month clubs, like Singles in Service and Community Impact, are just vehicles to enable people to give time or money as a package to "hot" causes. And business bandwagons, like Broadway Cares and Design Industries Foundation for AIDS, enable members of trade associations to contribute to causes under the flag of "involved industry." (In some cases, there is a natural business reason — e.g., publishers and libraries are directly affected by literacy.)

These groups *can* contribute positively to solving social problems. However, in both cases, it seems that spending time with your fellow volunteers or donors is more important than the cause itself.

Before starting a new organization, try an interim solution first: Begin a special interest group or division within an established nonprofit organization. Or search thoroughly for another organization in the same category whose philosophy or methods are more compatible with yours. Bigger is not always better, and you may feel that the larger, established organization's methods are wrong or wasteful.

Keep in mind that the costs in time and money of creating a new organization (applying for nonprofit status, distributing publicity, designing a logo, installing phone lines, etc.) are steep. The ongoing cost of maintaining a group (newsletters alone can use up a large chunk of time and money) also represents volunteer hours and dollars diverted from the main purpose of the organization.

Only if your idea is truly original — locally and nationally — and unacceptable to existing nonprofit organizations should you create a brand-new organization. By and large, creating a new organization is an unneccessary drain on resources.

Can You Get Paid for This?

Although college students are beginning to use volunteer work as a career training ground, many people (especially women) see the process of turning a volunteer job into a paid career as accidental and gradual. "I did not get involved with politics for any future gain. I wasn't primed with an agenda," says Jeanie Austin, who started as a volunteer many years ago and worked her way up to a paid position as elected co-chairman of the Republican National Committee.

In 1982, Margo Leathers started volunteering for the American Lung Association (ALA). For her first six months, she worked as a writer, producing brochures and annual reports. Then she accepted a part-time paid position as director of programs. By 1990, she was a salaried executive director for a county branch of the ALA.

Nancy O'Connell, a special events organizer, was promoted in a similar fashion by the Audubon Zoo in New Orleans, Louisiana: volunteer chair of the fund-raising committee in 1984, paid consultant in 1985, full-time development events coordinator in 1990.

Many volunteers make the transition from unpaid volunteering to paid employment. If you are interested in switching to a paying job in the nonprofit sector, you can contact ACCESS and subscribe to *Community Jobs* for listings of opportunities nationwide. (See *Resources.*)

A Word to the Wise

After 25 years as a volunteer event manager, Marion Denby transferred her meeting management skills to the professional arena, starting The Planned Event in Washington, DC. The transition has been very successful, but she says, "I'm still learning. As a volunteer chair, you have a lot of authority to make decisions. As a business, it's the same job, but you can't order your employers around; you must wait for them to make the decision."

Saying Goodbye

Phrase letters of resignation very carefully, especially if you are leaving over a fierce organizational dispute. Steer clear of slander and libel: Stick to proven fact. You may want to use a letter of resignation to leave a specific committee; again, use discretion if the split is antagonistic. (See Graphic 10.2, *Letter of Resignation.*)

Of course, if you really feel strongly about the dispute, make a public exit. Sometimes volunteer members pass out resignation speeches or letters to the media, in hopes of focusing attention on the organization's problems.

Quick, public quitting of a group was appropriate in the following situation, for example. "Prominent New Yorkers bought tickets ranging from $250 to $5,000 to attend the fund-raiser for UNICEF and a new charity called the Creo Fund for Children with AIDS. Total contributions came to $829,000. But soon after, the Creo Society admitted that just $74,000 — 9 percent of the total receipts — would go to the two charities; the rest would pay for extravagant expenses and a $90,000 fee for the event's organizers. A chagrined Patty Hearst Shaw immediately disassociated herself from the Creo Society. Two board members resigned." (*Working Woman*, December, 1989.)

Lee Iacocca was accused of conflict of interest when reporters discovered that he chaired both the fund-raising committee for the renovation of the Statue of Liberty, and the committee which decided how such money was spent. After this relationship was publicized by the media, he decided to resign from one of the committees. His resignation statement was carefully phrased and released to news agencies.

If you're becoming inactive because of personal problems, do not reveal the exact nature of your difficulty to your supervisor unless you're very comfortable with everyone's knowing about it. Private letters or conversations don't always stay private. People do gossip, especially in smaller organizations.

When you decide to change committees, or work on other projects within the same organization, sum up your work, and briefly discuss how your experiences will help in your new position.

Leaving on a Positive Note

A lot of volunteers find that the hardest part of quitting any organization is leaving behind friendships. You may realize: "If I decided to quit tomorrow, who would I see? Who would I talk to?" If you are leaving under innocuous circumstances, simply state that you will miss the organization and its members.

In today's mobile society, volunteer members may move several times during their adult lives. Each move is accompanied by a change in their volunteer associations. If you are moving, mention that you'll be attending meetings in your new neighborhood; if possible, ask for a letter of introduction. (See Graphic 3.4, *Letter of Recommendation*). Even national organizations admit that each regional group has its own flavor; not every volunteer stays in the same organization in a new area.

December 12, 1991

Dear Victoria,

As you know, we're moving to just outside Boulder, Colorado, in January. I'm really going to miss people here.

I've thoroughly enjoyed working with you and the other Friends of the Library. I think we accomplished a lot in our first two years. I'm especially proud of the Little Folks Literary Halloween party; not only did we raise more than $1,000 dollars, but all the kids had a really good time!

Since there isn't a Friends of the Library group in my new town, I intend to start a group out there. You'll be my inspiration.

Thanks,

Maureen Nickelby

P.S. I'll drop off the files next Tuesday, okay? Have a lovely Christmas.

Graphic 10.2 ♦ Letter of Resignation

Chapter 11

Profitable Philanthropy: Can a Corporation Care?

Although Joan Patterson of the Volunteer Exchange in San Jose, California, applauds the willingness of corporations to be involved in volunteering, she also believes that "public relations is *the* most important motivation for corporations who facilitate volunteering for their employees."

Many corporations represent philanthropic giving as a "benefit" to prospective employees. But when companies contribute funds to education, it represents a conscious *investment* in future workers.

When the Stride Rite Corporation donates to child-centered causes, you may well suspect that the executives at Stride Rite are trying to influence parental attitudes.

Sometimes the exchange is clear: The Little Tikes Company in Hudson, Ohio, features pictures of employees' children in catalogs and on packaging. Little Tikes saves model fees, and parents get a shot at fame for their offspring.

A tangled web of profit motives and tax incentives lies beneath most transactions between nonprofit and profit-making organizations. Arrangements wherein some portion of profits is funneled to nonprofit organizations, or nonprofit organizations buy services or products from profit-making companies, are complex.

Remember, all companies have their own self-interest at heart. What you're looking for (as explained in Chapter 9, *For Members Only*) is a win-win situation.

Who benefits — and by how much — is the deciding factor for conscientious consumers.

Is Corporate Charity a Sham?

In her groundbreaking book on philanthropy, *Charity Begins at Home: Generosity and Self-Interest Among the Philanthropic Elite*, Teresa Odendahl calls for "hard-nosed muckraking reporting of the charity scene." (See *Resources*.)

For example, a scathing article in the November/December 1990 *Ms.* magazine denounced the surplus food industry. "'Non-profit' food distribution, which started as a volunteer effort, has become a megabusiness. In the aggregate, tax incentives for corporations to distribute faultily packaged goods or out-of-date ones are *uncapped*. In other words, the sky is the limit, not only on tax breaks for items that previously had to be disposed of as garbage, but also on the cost of transporting them. Where once corporations paid carters to haul this trash to dumps, now U.S. citizens pay to ship it to food bank networks."

The article, entitled "Let Them Eat Oven Browner," also noted that in 1986, Second Harvest distributed over 17 million pounds of nonfood items, but less than 2 million pounds of pasta.

A similarly sarcastic article in *Mother Jones* (March/April, 1991) was called "Greenwash!" It reviewed several advertisements touting the environmental awareness and programs of various large corporations; each example was followed by a detailed discussion of the negative or anti-environmental actions of the company, such as oil spills, deforestation, and illegal hazardous waste disposal.

But Marjorie Kelly, disturbed by the tone of the article, argues a domino effect: that even lip service or halfway measures lead to changes in corporate behavior, and that corporate philanthropy and responsibility should be applauded, not criticized. "If a company considers it important to be seen as progressive, that's wonderful. The company's own pronouncements will serve as pressure to make sure actions follow. And their advertisements will up the ante for other corporations, making responsibility the norm in business." (*Business Ethics*, May/June, 1991.) The growth in membership in the Center for Corporate Relations seems to support Kelly's views: 12 companies in 1986, over 180 companies in 1991. (See *Resources*.)

Are You Directly Responsible for Indirect Contributions?

"On Thursday, this store will donate a significant percentage of the day's proceeds to a community organization. Mark that day as a special one to shop!" reads the ad in your newspaper. Warning flags should go up in your mind.

◆ Exactly how much is a significant percentage?

◆ Net or gross?

◆ And why isn't it stated outright?

◆ Is a minimum contribution from the store promised, even if business stays flat on that day?

◆ Is there a cap on the store's contribution, even if business booms on that day?

It may make more sense to contribute directly to the organization, if you feel the cause is worthy. And another facet of the discussion: if you usually shop at that store, realize that the donation to the organization by the store is counted as either a business expense or a charitable deduction, and is eventually reflected in the price you pay for items.

If you really disagree with the choice of organization, perhaps you should write a letter of protest to the store and stop doing business there.

Here's a related example of how *mixed* motives and outcomes can be. Suppose your local supermarket chain begins a "green lane" system. One lane is designated for shoppers who provide their own reused shopping bags.

Is this program good for the environment? Yes, because it reduces landfill waste. Is it good for the store? Yes, because the store saves the cost of supplying those bags. The store then donates two cents per reused bag to a disease charity. Is it good for the charity? Sure, because the charity receives a check without doing any work. Is it good for the store? Yes, because the store takes a tax break for charitable contributions. Is it bad for the charity? Maybe, because the charity is selling its name — and, in effect, a seal of approval to the store — for a program with no accountability and no direct connection to the organization's purpose. Is it good for the store? Sure, because the store receives a boost to its public image in the community.

Graphic 11.1 ♦ The Caring Corporation?

Freedom of Choice for Shareholders

Some people feel that, instead of funding corporate philanthropy programs, companies should give dividends directly to shareholders — for shareholders to distribute as they wish. As one Fortune 500 executive said, "Occasionally, not very often, you find stockholders who say that companies should not give any money to fix societal problems or encourage employees to volunteer. Because that isn't their job; their job is to maximize the return to shareholders." If you agree, and you are a shareholder in such a situation, you can vote at the annual meeting to stop contributions (or perhaps just stop contributions to certain organizations), or you can sell your stock.

Many firms now offer "ethical investment" services: Calvert Social Investment Fund, Ethical Investments, Franklin Research and Development Corporation, The Parnassus Fund, Pax World Fund, Progressive Asset Management, Progressive Securities Financial Services Corporation, Working Assets Money Fund. The Council on Economic Priorities' *Better World Investment Guide* can help you choose stock in companies according to their "social record." (See *Resources*.)

Find Out Where the Profits Go!

A companion book to the above, *Shopping for A Better World*, can help make sure that you don't contribute money to an environmental group, then nullify that contribution by purchasing goods from an environmentally dangerous company. (See *Resources*.)

John Corlett, an executive at Planned Parenthood of Greater Cleveland, Ohio, uses strong words as he cites a related example: "It's important to remember that Tom Monaghan, president of Domino's Pizza, supports the tactics of Operation Rescue — a terrorist organization which seeks to forcibly block women from entering reproductive-health clinics which provide birth control and abortion services. Mr. Monaghan also contributed funds to a successful Michigan ballot measure that denied state funds to poor women seeking an abortion. Mr. Monaghan has almost certainly funded his anti-choice projects through Domino's profits. So think twice before you call Domino's." (*The Chronicle of Philanthropy*, June, 1990.)

Is Your Organization Selling Out?

Sponsorships, product endorsements, and donations of goods and services usually come with strings attached, too. Even a simple ad page in your community theater's program can provoke controversy.

In a complex three-way deal, the Denver Children's Museum, the American Humane Association, and StarKist/9 Lives collaborated on a "Kids and Pets" booklet. What was the division of responsibility? The Humane Association kicked in $13,000; the museum produced the book and received $.40 of each $1.25 booklet price; and StarKist/9 Lives paid for printing and distributing 62,000 copies as premiums to veterinarians and customers. Who wins in this situation? Does anyone lose?

Should your organization accept free alcoholic beverages from Martini and Rossi for your fund-raising dance? If your group is a chapter of Mothers Against Drunk Driving, it may be easy to say no to such offers. But what if the gift is not so clearly out of the question? What if the offered items (crackers) are perfectly acceptable, but your research shows that the manufacturer is RJR Nabisco (a tobacco company) — and you volunteer for the American Cancer Society?

Where do you draw the line?

"I know a company recently that made an offer: Your charity can sponsor our open house, but you get the people to come, and you charge the people. The company wouldn't donate anything to the opening. The owner is getting that open house for nothing. And yes, $75 goes to the charity. But $75 gets spent for the owner, so that he can show his building off," says one long-time volunteer fund-raiser. "I don't think that's right; I would *not* be a part of that."

"Some organizations are tempted into commercialism," complains an Illinois volunteer. "I see a lot of product endorsement, and it bothers me."

As of 1991, British corporations could buy advertising space on the merit badges of the Boy Scouts of Britain. Is your bowling league willing to display a corporate logo on each jacket, in order to afford the jackets at all? Are you duty-bound to wear your company's T-shirt during the boat race, if they pay for the trophies? How about the "goodie bags" given out to convention participants? Or the free "brand-name food coupons" inserted in the back of your community cookbook? Or the complimentary paper and pens (embossed with the hotel's logo) placed onto each chair in a conference room? Are you comfortable being a captive audience for these advertising gimmicks? Do you feel that your organization is being adequately recompensed?

Corporate Involvement Can Be Confusing

As a volunteer, you may be supervised by a paid staff member of the organization, or supervise staff loaned by a local business. You could also become a paid staff member, or remain a volunteer while selling certain services or goods to a nonprofit organization.

Defining your roles, and keeping them separate, is crucial to maintaining good relationships.

Loaned Employees

As one company president explained, "When we support the United Way campaign in most communities now, we not only match employees' gifts, we loan executives for full-time help on the campaign." And he continues, "We really only give money to projects where our employees are involved — either as members of boards, or volunteers of some kind." So sometimes your paid work affects your volunteer work.

Changing a Volunteer into a Staff Member

Some volunteers use a volunteer job as a steppingstone to a professional position, sometimes even continuing in the same organization. In fact, you may have angled for the promotion. However, this change can be rough on you and your volunteer colleagues, especially if your unpaid position just became paid.

A change in job title and a short vacation between jobs are recommended, so that you come back fresh into the new position.

Some Things Don't Mix

Maybe your organization needs a new database created for membership records; you're the membership administrator — and your husband is a computer consultant. Or perhaps you're a public relations expert who currently volunteers as a tour guide, and your museum is searching for someone to produce the glossy annual report.

Take a piece of advice: Direct paid vendor relations with your organization are almost always a bad idea.

You can, of course, recommend people you know, or even friends. If the departments and tasks involved are quite separate (as in the public relations case above), a business relationship can work smoothly. However, it is hard to keep changing roles, especially if your volunteer job and your paid job are similar. Basically, the chances of problems, ill feeling, and mismanagement are too great. Entering into a long-term business association is liable to backfire, especially if services are the purchased product. And such arrangements can lead to even more trouble: Members and outside investigators may claim conflict of interest.

If you simply want to contribute a much-needed piece of used equipment from your storeroom, do so. If you are able, through industry contacts, to obtain supplies at wholesale prices, that can be arranged to the satisfaction of all parties. In both cases, make sure that the proper tax forms and receipts are filed and approved.

To avoid any appearance of double-dealing, abstain from voting on any issue where you are financially concerned.

Chapter 12

The Pitfalls of Volunteering: 1,000 Points of Darkness?

In the last five years, I've discovered some disturbing trends in the nonprofit world.

Volunteering is a hot media topic in the 90s, but mostly in an uncritical, "do good, feel good" atmosphere. Volunteering your time and money is *automatically* accepted and promoted as a good thing — for you, for society, for the recipients of such charity.

It's not necessarily so.

The most important ethical dilemma for a volunteer is whether to give time or donate money at all. Smart volunteers know when to say *no*, for their own good and the good of the organization. Carefully assess each commitment before you make it. (See Graphic 12.1, *Should You Do It?*)

Is the Project Right for the Organization?

One of the most neglected steps in volunteering is to evaluate the need for the project before volunteering.

Stop to think.

Does this program serve your organization's *purpose*? Will this program or project further the goals of your group? Have you evaluated alternative proposals?

Graphic 12.1 ♦ **Should You Do It?**

Fred Davie was upset at what he saw, not only as competition, but also as contradictions in the activities of libraries in Tacoma, Washington. "I operate a video store in a community in which our tax-supported library provides the same tapes for free. While rental prices in our city are not unreasonably high, librarians are feverishly expanding their video catalog to meet the demand caused by unexplained video store failures. Since the provision of these tapes encourages an increasingly illiterate community to spend even less time reading, one might think that the library is operating in direct conflict with its avowed purpose." (*INC.*, December, 1987.)

The Ultimate Purpose

"If nonprofit organizations were ultimately successful," notes Joyce Hatton Yarrow, president of the Institute for Nonprofit Training and Development in Hartford, Connecticut, "they would go out of business." And a highly committed Harvard University student activist goes even further: "Public service organizations *should* be putting themselves out of business; that should be their goal." This is not relevant, of course, to all organizations (educational and social clubs, for example), since some are formed to provide permanent activities, not permanent solutions.

"Loser" Activities

I love buying cupcakes at bake sales and reading those cute spiral-bound "community cookbooks," but I always suffer moral qualms, because my experience tells me that, with few exceptions, such fund-raising projects take much too much volunteer time and effort — for too little return.

For example, your church choir is trying to raise funds for new robes. The members decide to use a bake sale to raise funds. Twenty volunteers work on the bake sale. Sixteen of you spend approximately $3 each on ingredients and $1\frac{1}{2}$ hours each baking. You spend 2 hours drawing, photocopying, and distributing posters and signs, at a cost of $4. One person spends an hour picking up, pricing, and labeling the goods (labels and gasoline, $2). The remaining two volunteers staff a table, selling baked goods and collecting money for 3 hours.

Total time investment is 33 hours. Total costs of materials is $54. Total income is $112. "Profit" is $58, or approximately $3 per person.

However, look at this another way. Each person "contributed" approximately $3 in ingredients *and* $1\frac{1}{2}$ hours of work (which "earned" less than $2/hour). If each member had simply kicked in $6 and no time, the income would be the same.

Unless your group lists other goals for the bake sale (publicity or camaraderie), refuse to take part in a bake sale.

Here is a closely related example: a cookbook produced by a parent-teacher group in Mandeville, Louisiana. "It took about four months to collect and organize 480 recipes from about 300 families. In the first two months they sold 350 for $9 each. About 50% of that was profit." (*Changing Times*, July, 1989.) The marketing of such a book requires some ongoing volunteer work, but at least this group — unlike the bake sale group — has a renewable, tangible product.

Frequently, however, such cookbooks or organization yearbooks result in a tidy profit to the printer, while each member who contributes and/or is mentioned in the book buys one or two books at more than production cost. This might be an enjoyable project for friends or family, but the total monetary gain for the organization is *not* enough to justify the amount of volunteer time and organization support required.

As I pointed out in *Organizing Special Events and Conferences*, "A rule of thumb is that such events should gross three to four times their cost (if your costs are zero because of sponsors, you'll end up making more than that)." (See *Resources*.)

All projects deserve close examination. Although a common problem with many fund-raising projects is not thinking big enough, the problem with other kinds of proposals (not intended to raise funds) is thinking too big.

For example, are there compelling reasons to switch your organization's quarterly newsletter to a monthly magazine? Do these reasons justify the increase in volunteer effort and expense? Analyze the pros and cons. Try invoking some of the "Ingredients of Compromise" listed in Chapter 6, *Powerful Problems and Petty Politics*.

Is the Project Right for You?

Perhaps you agree with the volunteer who says, "I would probably feel guilty if I could help something, and I didn't." But always consider your personal goals. If the volunteer work is more boring or distasteful than useful, or if it doesn't improve or use your skills, say no.

Are Your Motives Pure?

Although a literacy volunteer from Pennsylvania, tutor to a man named Bud, believes that your motivation must be selfless — "How do you think Bud, or any recipient of volunteerism, would feel if our time was based on a desire to improve the contents of a résumé?" (*U.S. News & World Report*, May 15, 1989) — many volunteers and nonprofit experts agree that "There is no such thing as an altruistic volunteer."

Make sure that your volunteer work is giving you what you want and need, whether it's a credit line on your résumé or the glow of "helping someone who's worse off than me."

You Want Me to Do What?

You may find yourself with a moral dilemma. What if, as happened in Massachusetts, your temple urges members to fill in for absent Christian volunteers in hospitals and senior centers during December? Your duties would include serving ham dinners and distributing Christmas presents. Do you volunteer?

Is the Timing Good for You?

Always estimate the number of hours a project or position will need in advance (use the schedules in Chapter 4, *Your Résumé*), and make your decision based on that information. Schedule conflicts — an exam at the peak commitment time, big projects at work, a bad fit with school vacation time for your children — are clear signals to say no.

Full-time employees should limit time contributions for nonprofit organizations to some portion of available leisure hours; *never* use business time to complete volunteer assignments. Instead, ask your supervisor to "donate" your time and services, or to allow you flexible hours.

Are You Stealing Someone Else's Job?

"Volunteers are not cheap labor!" cautions Carolyn Losos. And Patrick Shannon, director of volunteer services at the University of Chicago Hospitals, warns, "If a hospital is somewhat exploitative, what they actually try to do is replace paid workers with volunteers. Volunteers should watch out for that."

All Members Are Not Created Equal

Can only rich people volunteer? "It isn't the secretary who's rushing home to get to her child's Cub Scout meeting, or a Greenpeace meeting, or church ladies' group meeting, who gets any time off. It's the junior executive who's given the afternoon off to plan a charity ball with other junior executives," one volunteer noted angrily.

"It has long been an expected part of a board member's role that he or she make a significant donation to the organization. The theory behind this principle is that a generous contribution by a board member indicates a true interest and belief in the organization's purpose." (*The Responsibilities of a Charity's Volunteer Board*, Philanthropic Advisory Service of the Council of Better Business Bureaus.) (See *Resources*.) Professional fund-raisers also insist that volunteers who solicit donations should have contributed at least as much as they are asking the individual prospect to contribute. This tradition has led to accusations that board members must buy their seats on boards.

Some supporters of multiculturalism also charge that this technique prevents minority and low-income people from joining boards and changing policies to open up the organization's viewpoint or activities. A few organizations, notably women's groups, recruit clients (people who receive assistance or services from the organization) to be board members.

The National Committee for Responsive Philanthropy (NCRP) is concerned about the lack of philanthropic giving to new organizations working for social change or progressive issues, the lack of public accountability, and the giving patterns of private foundations, of United Way International, and of corporations with philanthropic programs. Women and Foundations/Corporate Philanthropy (WFCP) also probes these issues. (See *Resources*.)

Are Volunteers Second-class Citizens?

Perhaps your trade association, like many, refuses to take volunteers seriously — won't allow volunteers to join, won't evaluate volunteer experience for professional certification, won't include programming directed at volunteers. It's a short-sighted policy, given how many people choose careers as a result of volunteer work. Further, these volunteers could be a lucrative new target market for associations. And wouldn't members' professional pride include sharing knowledge and teaching people? Does it matter if these people are not getting paid for their work? Does that devalue it?

Can Volunteering Be Involuntary?

Can you be *forced* to volunteer? Whether you're a student or employee, the trend toward mandatory volunteering should alarm you.

Would You Rather Go to Jail?

Clark Kent Ervin, of the Office of National Service, sums up his ambivalence: "We are always of two minds when judges sentence people to community service — when an Ollie North or a Rob Lowe is sentenced to community service. Because on the one hand, we support any mechanism that gets people involved in community service. On the other hand, that sends the message that community service is a penalty." Many nonprofit sector experts are opposed "because it equates volunteerism with punishment."

And class issues are raised when celebrities, such as Zsa Zsa Gabor, are sentenced to community service, while poor urban minority youths are sentenced to jail — for equivalent crimes.

Big Brother Is Watching You

In early 1991, the White House instituted procedures to collect information on volunteer activities of government employees.

In the private sector, perhaps your company, like many, has established a community liaison or service office. Activities of such departments can include tracking volunteer efforts, recognizing and awarding employees' volunteer service, posting volunteer opportunities, providing free training, and contributing money or goods to nonprofit organizations.

In the 1987 J.C. Penney/VOLUNTEER survey, 60% of those employees who were encouraged by their employer did volunteer work. The minimum benefit to a corporation from donating people to a nonprofit organization is positive public relations. Why do you think Hitachi America purchased a full page in *INC.* magazine to talk about the company's philanthropy program?

When you participate in volunteer efforts organized and/or endorsed by your company, remember that your company is, in effect, getting credit for *your* private life.

Big Brother Is Asking You

Certain kinds of employees, usually management, are expected to volunteer with specific organizations as part of climbing the executive ladder.

"Some companies are actually writing in job descriptions that they expect the employee to volunteer time for some community projects," reports Donald W. Davis, Chairman of the Board, Stanley Works. "This is typically true of banks and insurance companies or utilities who are relying on the local communities as customers. Their consciousness about problems in the community is obviously very high. I know a number of companies now that, when they set up the incentive programs for executives, include certain societal objectives in their targets for the year — whether it be affirmative action in hiring, or a certain number of employees doing volunteer work."

Big Brother Is Telling You

Pauline Kezer notes one of the key questions for educators today. "Should we change the curriculum? Should we mandate that curriculums include a service component, so that every child who goes to school gets to learn and experience being a volunteer?"

Educators are developing community service curriculums for students. Dennis Smith, of the United States Department of Education, researched this phenomenon, and reports: "In Atlanta and Detroit, for example, high school students are expected to do 200 hours of volunteer work during their four years of high school.

In Washington, DC, junior and high school students are required to perform 100 hours of community service in order to graduate from high school. In Chicago, students are given elective credits for hospital volunteer work."

He continues, "In Maryland, schools were given a grant by the ABLE foundation to increase public school students' volunteer activity. They developed a pilot program. Students could take a course — just as they would sign up for algebra, or economics, or English — scheduled at the end of the day that involved volunteer work. Four days a week, they would leave school early and do their volunteer work. On the fifth day, they would attend a seminar to discuss what they were doing. They received regular course credit. In 1985, Maryland became the first state that required schools to offer courses for credit that involved volunteer work."

The Next Step

If the National Association for Public Interest Law is successful, community service will be a required part of every law student's education by the year 2000.

A flurry of bills about "national service" presented to Congress in 1990 resulted in the passage of the National and Community Service Act. While this legislation falls short of *requiring* community service, political experts note individual efforts by states to encourage or demand voluntary service. Future action on the national level is predicted. (See Graphic 12.2, *Is This Progress?*)

It's a disturbingly short road (paved with good intentions, surely) from noting, to praising, to facilitating — to demanding — volunteer participation, isn't it?

Will this be the future? We'll have to wait and see . . .

Graphic 12.2 ♦ Is This Progress?

Part Six

Resources

Appendix A

Books and Booklets

Part One
Where Do You Fit?

Carroll, Andrew, *Volunteer USA*, Fawcett Columbine, New York, NY, 1991.

Council on International Educational Exchange, *Volunteer! The Comprehensive Guide to Voluntary Service in the U.S. and Abroad*, CIEE, New York, NY, 1992.

Ellis, Susan J., and Noyes, Katherine H., *By the People: A History of Americans as Volunteers*, Jossey-Bass Inc. Publishers, San Francisco, CA, 1990.

McMillon, Bill, *Volunteer Vacations: A Directory of Short-Term Adventures That Will Benefit You . . . and Others*, Chicago Review Press, Chicago, IL, 1991.

Meisel, Wayne, and Hackett, Robert, *Building a Movement: A Resource Book for Students in Community Service*, Campus Outreach Opportunity League, Minneapolis, MN, 1986.

Part Two
Join Today, New Job Tomorrow

Devney, Darcy Campion, *Organizing Special Events and Conferences: A Practical Guide for Busy Volunteers and Staff*, Pineapple Press, Sarasota, FL, 1990.

Driver, David, *The Good Heart Book: A Guide to Volunteering*, The Noble Press, Chicago, IL, 1989.

Flanagan, Joan, *Successful Fundraising: A Complete Handbook for Volunteers and Professionals*, Contemporary Books, Chicago, IL, 1991.

Lawrence, Elizabeth, *The Complete Caterer: A Practical Guide to the Craft and Business of Being a Caterer*, Doubleday, New York, NY, 1988.

Ramacitti, David F., *Do-It-Yourself Publicity*, Amacom, New York, NY, 1990.

Raynolds, John F. and Eleanor, *Beyond Success: How Volunteer Service Can Help You Begin Making a Life Instead of Just a Living*, Master Media Ltd., New York, NY, 1988.

Wilson, Marlene, *You Can Make a Difference: Helping Yourself and Others Through Volunteering*, Volunteer Management Associates, Boulder, CO, 1990.

Part Three
Savvy Networking

Adams, Tom, *Grass Roots: How Ordinary People are Changing America*, Citadel Press, New York, NY, 1991.

Baber, Anne, and Wayman, Lynne, *Great Connections: Small Talk and Networking for Businesspeople*, Impact Publications, Woodbridge, VA, 1991.

Martin, Judith, *Miss Manners' Guide for the Turn-of-the-Millenium*, Pharos Books, New York, NY, 1989.

Sher, Barbara, and Gottlieb, Annie, *Teamworks! Building Support Groups that Guarantee Success*, Warner Books, New York, NY, 1989.

Sonte, Bonnie Domrose, and Alt, Betty Sowers, *Uncle Sam's Brides: The World of Military Wives*, Walker & Company, New York, NY, 1990.

Part Four
What Do You Give, What Do You Get?

Cahn, Edgar S., *The Time Dollar*, Essential Information, Washington, DC, 1990.

Ekstrom, Ruth B., *How to Get College Credit for What You Have Learned as a Homemaker and Volunteer*, Educational Testing Service, Princeton, NJ.

Gershen, Howard, *A Guide for Giving: 250 Charities and How They Use Your Money*, Pantheon Books, New York, NY, 1990.

Independent Sector, *How Much Really Is Tax-Deductible?* Independent Sector, Washington, DC, 1989.

Kipps, Harriet Clyde, editor, *Volunteerism: The Directory of Organizations, Training, Programs, and Publications (Third Edition)*, R.R. Bowker, New Providence, NJ, 1991.

Weisbrod, Burton, *The Nonprofit Economy*, Harvard University Press, Cambridge, MA, 1988.

Part Five
A Volunteer's Dilemmas

The Council on Economic Priorities, *Better World Investment Guide*, Prentice-Hall, New York, NY, 1991.

The Council on Economic Priorities, *Shopping for a Better World: A Quick and Easy Guide to Socially Responsible Supermarket Shopping*, Ballantine Books, New York, NY, 1991.

Doble, John, with Richardson, Amy and Danks, Allen, *Public Opinion About Charitable Solicitation and the Law*, Public Agenda Foundation, New York, NY, 1990.

Odendahl, Teresa, *Charity Begins at Home: Generosity and Self-Interest Among the Philanthropic Elite*, Basic Books, New York, NY, 1990.

Appendix B

Organizations

ACCESS: Networking in the Public Interest
50 Beacon St., Boston, MA 02108.
Phone: (617) 720-5627.
Publishes: *Community Jobs* (monthly newspaper).

American Society of Association Executives (ASAE)
1575 Eye St. NW, Washington, DC 20005.
Phone: (202) 626-2748.
Publishes: *Association Management* (monthly magazine);
Leadership (annual magazine).

Association for Research on Nonprofit Organizations and Voluntary Action (ARNOVA)
Route 2, Box 696, Pullman, WA 99163.
Phone: (509) 332-3417.
Publishes: *Nonprofit Voluntary Sector Quarterly* (quarterly journal).

Association for Volunteer Administration (AVA)
P.O. Box 4584, Boulder, CO 80306.
Phone: (303) 541-0238.
Publishes: *AVA Update* (bimonthly newsletter).

Break Away: the Alternative Break Connection
Box 18, Peabody Campus, Vanderbilt Univ., Nashville, TN 37203.
Phone: (615) 343-0385.
Publishes: *Connections* (quarterly newsletter).

California Association of Hospitals and Health Systems (CAHHS)
Volunteer Services Division, P.O. Box 2038, Sacramento,
CA 95812-2038.
Phone: (916) 552-7505.
Publishes: *Volunteer Recognition Catalog* (annual catalog).

Call for Action, Inc.
3400 Idaho Ave. NW, Ste. 101, Washington, DC 20016.
Phone: (202) 537-0585.
Publishes: *Network News* (quarterly newsletter).

Calvert Social Investment Fund
4550 Montgomery Ave., Ste. 1000N, Bethesda, MD 20814.
Phone: (800) 368-2750 or (301) 951-4814.

Campus Outreach Opportunity League (COOL)
University of Minnesota, 386 McNeal Hall, St. Paul,
MN 55108-1011.
Phone: (612) 624-3018.
Publishes: *Campus Outreach* (5/year newsletter).

The Center for Corporate Community Relations
Boston College, 16 College Rd., Chestnut Hill, MA 02167-3835.
Phone: (617) 552-4545.
Publishes: *Corporate Community Relations Letter* (monthly
newsletter).

Center for Nonprofit Excellence
3003 E. Third Ave., Ste. 105, Denver, CO 80206.
Phone: (303) 399-3253.

Council for Advancement and Support of Education (CASE)
11 Dupont Circle, Ste. 400, Washington, DC 20036.
Phone: (202) 328-5900.
Publishes: *Currents* (10/year magazine).

Council on Economic Priorities (CEP)
30 Irving Pl., New York, NY 10003.
Phone: (212) 420-1133.
Publishes: *CEP Research Report* (monthly newsletter).

Council on International Educational Exchange (CIEE)
205 E. Forty-second St., New York, NY 10017.
Phone: (212) 661-1414.
Publishes: *Campus Update* (11/year newsletter).

Development and Technical Assistance Center, Inc. (DATA)
70 Audubon St., New Haven, CT 06510.
Phone: (800) 788-5598.
Publishes: *Successful Nonprofits* (quarterly newsletter).

Ethical Investments
430 First Ave. N., Ste. 204, Minneapolis, MN 55401.
Phone: (612) 339-3939.

Four-One-One (411)
7304 Beverly St., Annandale, VA 22003.
Phone: (703) 354-6270.
Publishes: *Mirror on Volunteerism* (3/year newsletter);
  Super Volunteers!/Small World Journal (quarterly journal).

Franklin Research and Development Corporation
711 Atlantic Ave., Boston, MA 02111.
Phone: (800) 548-5684 or (617) 423-6655.
Publishes: *Insight* (monthly newsletter).

Friends of Libraries U.S.A. (FOLUSA)
50 E. Huron St., Chicago, IL 60611.
Phone: (215) 790-1674.
Publishes: *Idea Bank* (quarterly newsletter);
  Friends of Libraries U.S.A. National Notebook (quarterly newsletter).

Global Volunteers
375 E. Little Canada Rd., St. Paul, MN 55117.
Phone: (612) 482-1074 or (800) 487-1074.
Publishes: *Global Volunteers* (2/year newsletter).

Independent Sector (IS)
1828 L St. NW, Washington, DC 20036.
Phone: (202) 223-8100.

Indiana University Center on Philanthropy
550 W. North St., Ste. 301, Indianapolis, IN 46202-3162.
Phone: (800) 962-6692 or (314) 274-7063.
Publishes: *Philanthropic Studies Index* (quarterly booklet);
  Research in Progress in Philanthropy (annual booklet).

Institute for Nonprofit Training and Development, Inc.
Hartford Graduate Ctr., 275 Windsor St., Hartford, CT 06120-2991.
Phone: (203) 548-7811.

Internal Revenue Service (IRS)
1111 Constitution Ave. NW, Washington, DC 20224.
Phone: (202) 566-6208.
Publishes: *Charitable Contributions* (#526);
  Determining the Value of Donated Property (#561);
  Deductibility of Payments Made to Charities Conducting Fund-Raising Events (#1391).

Mandel Center for Nonprofit Organizations
Case Western Reserve Univ., 10900 Euclid Ave., Cleveland, OH 44106.
Phone: (216) 368-2275.
Publishes: *Nonprofit Notes* (quarterly newsletter).

National Association for Campus Activities (NACA)
13 Harbison Way, Columbia, SC 29212.
Phone: (803) 732-6222.
Publishes: *Campus Activities Programming* (9/year magazine);
Leadership (monthly newsletter);
Profile (monthly newsletter).

National Charities Information Bureau (NCIB)
19 Union Square W., Sixth Floor, New York, NY 10003.
Phone: (212) 929-6300.
Publishes: *Wise Giving Guide* (3/year booklet).

National Committee for Responsive Philanthropy (NCRP)
2001 S St. NW, Ste. 620, Washington, DC 20009.
Phone: (202) 387-9177.
Publishes: *Responsive Philanthropy* (quarterly newsletter).

The NATIONAL Volunteer Center
Points of Light Foundation, 1111 N. Nineteenth St., Ste. 500,
Arlington, VA 22209.
Phone: (703) 276-0542.
Publishes: *Volunteering* (bimonthly newsletter);
Voluntary Action Leadership (quarterly magazine);
Volunteer Readership (annual catalog).

Office of National Service
The White House, Washington, DC 20500.
Phone: (202) 456-6266.

The Other Side
300 West Apsley St., Philadelphia, PA 19144.
Phone: (212) 849-2178.
Publishes: *The Other Side* (bimonthly magazine).

The Parnassus Fund
244 California St., San Francisco, CA 94111.
Phone: (800) 999-3505 or (415) 362-3505.

Pax World Fund
224 State St., Portsmouth, NH 03801.
Phone: (800) 767-1729 or (603) 431-8022.

Philanthropic Advisory Service (PAS)
Council of Better Business Bureaus, 4200 Wilson Blvd., Arlington,
VA 22203.
Phone: (703) 276-0100.
Publishes: *Give . . . But Give Wisely* (bimonthly booklet);
Annual Charity Index (yearly book).

Program on Nonprofit Organizations
Yale Univ., Yale Station Box 154, 88 Trumbull St., New Haven, CT 06520-0154.
Phone: (203) 432-2121.
Publishes: *Research Reports* (annual newsletter).

Progressive Asset Management
1814 Franklin St., Ste. 710, Oakland, CA 94612.
Phone: (800) 786-2998 or (415) 834-3722.
Publishes: *Progressive Investment News* (quarterly newsletter).

Progressive Securities Financial Services Corporation
2435 SW Fifth Ave., Portland, OR 97201.
Phone: (800) 776-4737 or (503) 224-7828.
Publishes: *Progressive Securities Newsletter* (quarterly newsletter).

Public Agenda Foundation
6 E. Thirty-ninth St., New York, NY 10016.
Phone: (212) 686-6610.
Publishes: *America's Agenda* (quarterly newsletter).

Retired Senior Volunteer Program, ACTION
1100 Vermont Ave. NW, Washington, DC 20525.
Phone: (202) 606-4853.
Publishes: *Insight* (quarterly newsletter).

Service Corps of Retired Executives (SCORE)
409 Third St. SW, Ste. 5900, Washington, DC 20024-3213.
Phone: (202) 205-6762.
Publishes: *The Savant* (monthly newsletter).

Society for Nonprofit Organizations
6314 Odana Rd., Ste. 1, Madison, WI 53719.
Phone: (608) 274-9777.
Publishes: *Nonprofit World* (bimonthly magazine).

Studies of Voluntarism and Social Participation, Inc. (SVSP)
P.O. Box 1495, Alpine, TX 79831.
Phone: (915) 837-2930.
Publishes: *Voluntarism Review and Reporter* (2/year journal).

Support Centers of America
2001 O St. NW, Washington, DC 20036.
Phone: (202) 296-3900.
Publishes: *Management Workshops for Nonprofits* (3/year catalog).

Toastmasters International
23182 Arroyo Vista, Rancho Santa Margarita, CA 92688.
Phone: (714) 858-8255.
Publishes: *The Toastmaster* (monthly magazine).

United Way of America
 701 N. Fairfax St., Alexandria, VA 22314.
 Phone: (703) 836-7100.
 Publishes: *Executive Newsletter* (weekly newsletter);
  Perspective (quarterly newsletter).

Women and Foundations/Corporate Philanthropy (WFCP)
 322 Eighth Ave., New York, NY 10001.
 Phone: (212) 463-9934.
 Publishes: *Women and Foundations Newsletter* (3/year newsletter).

Working Assets Money Fund
 230 California St., Ste. 500, San Francisco, CA 94111-9865.
 Phone: (800) 533-3863 or (415) 989-3200.
 Publishes: *Money Matters* (quarterly newsletter).

Appendix C

Magazines and Periodicals

Arts Management (5/year newsletter)
408 W. Fifty-seventh St., New York, NY 10019.
Phone: (212) 245-3850.

Business Ethics (bimonthly magazine)
1107 Hazeltine Blvd., Ste. 530, Chaska, MN 55318.
Phone: (612) 448-8864.

Campus Activities Programming (9/year magazine)
National Association for Campus Activities (NACE), 13 Harbison
Way, Columbia, SC 29212.
Phone: (803) 732-6222.

Changing Times (bimonthly section, "Giving Back")
1729 H St. NW, Washington, DC 20006.
Phone: (202) 887-6400.

Channels (monthly newsletter)
PR Publishing Co., P.O. Box 600, Exeter, NH 03833.
Phone: (603) 778-0514.

The Chronicle of Philanthropy (biweekly newspaper)
1255 Twenty-Third St. NW, Ste. 775, Washington, DC 20037.
Phone: (202) 466-1200.

Church Media Library Magazine (quarterly magazine)
Baptist Sunday School Board, 127 Ninth Ave. N., Nashville,
TN 37234.
Phone: (800) 458-2772.

Community Jobs (monthly newspaper)
ACCESS, 50 Beacon St., Boston, MA 02108.
Phone: (617) 720-5627.

Contributions (bimonthly newspaper)
  634 Commonwealth Ave., Ste. 201, Newton Center, MA 02159.
  Phone: (617) 964-2688.

Cooking for Profit (monthly magazine)
  104 S. Main St., #717, P.O. Box 267, Fond du Lac, WI 54936-0267.
  Phone: (414) 923-3700.

Free Materials for Schools and Libraries (5/year newsletter)
  Dyad Services, Box C34069, Dept. 284, Seattle, WA 98124-1069.
  Phone: (604) 734-0255.

Fund Raising Management (monthly magazine)
  Hoke Communications, 224 Seventh St., Garden City,
    NY 11530-5771.
  Phone: (516) 746-6700.

Grapevine (bimonthly newsletter)
  Heritage Arts, 1807 Prairie Ave., Downers Grove, IL 60515.
  Phone: (708) 964-1194.

Grassroots Fundraising Journal (bimonthly newsletter)
  Klein & Honig Partnership, P.O. Box 11607, Berkeley, CA 94701.
  Phone: (212) 673-6216.

Meeting News (monthly magazine)
  Gralla Publications, 1515 Broadway, New York, NY 10036.
  Phone: (212) 869-1300.

Nonprofit Issues (monthly newsletter)
  Montgomery, McCracken, Walker, and Rhoads, Three Pkwy.,
    Philadelphia, PA 19102.
  Phone: (215) 665-7554.

Nonprofit Management and Leadership (quarterly journal)
  Jossey-Bass Inc. Publishers, 350 Sansome St., San Francisco,
    CA 94104.
  Phone: (415) 433-1767.

Nonprofit Management Strategies (monthly newsletter)
  The Taft Group, 12300 Twinbrook Pkwy., Ste. 450, Rockville,
    MD 20853.
  Phone: (301) 816-0210.

The NonProfit Times (monthly newspaper)
  190 Tamarack Circle, Skillman, NJ 08558.
  Phone: (609) 921-1251.

Nonprofit World (bimonthly magazine)
  Society for Nonprofit Organizations, 6314 Odana Rd., Ste. 1,
    Madison, WI 53719.
  Phone: (608) 274-9777.

Philanthropy Monthly (10/year magazine)
P.O. Box 989, New Milford, CT 06776.
Phone: (203) 354-7132.

Successful Meetings (monthly magazine)
Bill Communications, 633 Third Ave., New York, NY 10017.
Phone: (212) 986-4800.

Successful Nonprofits (quarterly newsletter)
Development and Technical Assistance Center, Inc. (DATA),
70 Audubon St., New Haven, CT 06510.
Phone: (800) 788-5598.

The Toastmaster (monthly magazine)
Toastmasters International, 23182 Arroyo Vista, Rancho Santa
Margarita, CA 92688.
Phone: (714) 858-8255.

Voluntarism Review and Reporter (2/year journal)
Studies of Voluntarism and Social Participation, Inc. (SVSP),
P.O. Box 1495, Alpine, TX 79831.
Phone: (915) 837-2930.

Volunteer Action Leadership (quarterly magazine)
The NATIONAL Volunteer Center, Points of Light Foundation,
1111 N. Nineteenth St., Ste. 500, Arlington, VA 22209.
Phone: (703) 276-0542.

Volunteer Energy Resource Catalog, 1991–1992 (annual catalog)
Energize, Inc., 5450 Wissahickon Ave., Philadelphia, PA 19144.
Phone: (215) 438-8342 or (800) 395-9800.

Volunteering (bimonthly newsletter)
The NATIONAL Volunteer Center, Points of Light Foundation,
1111 N. Nineteenth St., Ste. 500, Arlington, VA 22209.
Phone: (703) 276-0542.

Volunteer Marketplace (annual catalog)
Heritage Arts, 1807 Prairie Ave., Downers Grove, IL 60515.
Phone: (708) 964-1194.

Volunteer Readership (annual catalog)
The NATIONAL Volunteer Center, Points of Light Foundation,
1111 North Nineteenth St., Ste. 500, Arlington, VA 22209.
Phone: (703) 276-0542.

Volunteer Recognition Catalog (annual catalog)
California Association of Hospitals and Health Systems (CAHHS),
Volunteer Services Division, P.O. Box 2038, Sacramento,
CA 95812-2038.
Phone: (916) 552-7505.

Volunteer Today (bimonthly newsletter)
Macduff/Bunt Associates, 821 Lincoln St., Walla Walla, WA 99362.
Phone: (509) 529-0244.

Volunteer Vacations Update (quarterly newsletter)
2120 Green Hill Rd., Sebastopol, CA 95472.
Phone: (707) 829-9364.

Index

Organizing
Special Events & Conferences:
A Practical Guide for Busy
Volunteers & Staff

*"For organizations that rely on volunteers to plan
everything from small church socials to fundraisers for
thousands, Devney's text is a goldmine of information."*

(*Booklist*, American Library Association)

Softcover 8½x11 ♦ 129 pages ♦ ISBN 0-910923-63-9

Order today! $16.95

Add $2 postage & handling per book.
(In Massachusetts, add $.85 sales tax per book.)
Bulk purchase discounts available.

Send your check to :
The Practical Press, Dept BB, P.O. Box 2296, Cambridge, MA 02238.

Do You Need . . .
Your own copy of this book?
A copy for your organization?
A gift for a friend who volunteers?

The Volunteer's Survival Manual:
The Only Practical Guide to
Giving Your Time and Money

One Reviewer's Comments

"As a former volunteer administrator and current teacher of individuals interested in finding their perfect niche in the volunteer world, I can sincerely and knowledgeably say that it is certainly time for a consumer's guide to volunteer work. I heartily second your perspective that individuals need to carefully evaluate their options as volunteers, in the same way that a wise consumer would comparison shop.

"I found that the book offered many words of wisdom, as well as many provocative ideas . . .

"You have undertaken an extremely large and somewhat controversial task, that of advising us how to judiciously parse out our valuable spare moments to serve others and simultaneously help ourselves. I applaud your effort and hope that many potential and current volunteers will read the book."

(Nancy Kressin, lifelong volunteer)

Softcover 6x9 ♦ 192 pages ♦ ISBN 0-9630686-9-5

Order today! $15.95

Add $2 postage & handling per book.
(In Massachusetts, add $.80 sales tax per book.)
Bulk purchase discounts available.

Send your check to :
The Practical Press, Dept BB, P.O. Box 2296, Cambridge, MA 02238.

Acknowledgments

I was astonished anew at the willingness of total strangers to open up their lives and share their thoughts. Nonfiction writers depend on such people to add sparkle to a book. Besides, I really enjoyed talking with each of you and learning about your projects. Thanks again to: Barbara Beckwith, Rich Braun, Carl E. Cookson, Sheryl Fitzgibbon, Lelia Fykes-Ridley, Virginia E. McCullough, Joan Patterson, Michael Kelley Potter, Dave Schwartz, and Patrick Shannon.

Volunteers and professionals from many organizations answered my questions and sent materials: Betty Baker (United Way), Sue Chenoweth (*San Jose Mercury News*), David Day (National Park Service), Jeff Gingerich (United Telephone System), Tom Griffin (Griffin Insurance Agency), Julie M. Halpern (Hyatt Hotels Corp.), Susan Karkoska (Dublin-McCarter and Associates), Michael Levine (Levine/Schneider Public Relations), Cheryl Martin (Council for Advancement and Support of Education), Charlotte A. Rancilio (American Optometric Association), Ricki F. Wasserman (Queens Borough Public Library), Leigh Weimers (*San Jose Mercury News*), Betty Yarmon (*PartyLine*). And comments from Karin Murphy (Harvard Business School Press), Joseph O'Malley, and Michael A. Devney were very helpful.

I am especially grateful to Ms. Pauline Kezer, leader of a study group called "Voluntarism in the 90s: Reviving the Call to Public Service" at the Institute of Politics, Harvard University. Ms. Kezer and her guest speakers provided a wealth of information and anecdotes about volunteering, and the students posed some thought-provoking questions that helped to shape this book. Thanks again to: Jeanie Austin, Susan B. Butler, Donald W. Davis, Clark Kent Ervin, Carolyn W. Losos, Carolyn Neal, Dennis R. Smith, Joyce Hatton Yarrow.

The production of a book requires a team of professionals: Robert E. Devney was a constant editorial inspiration; Cassandra Boell's illustrations gracefully convey difficult concepts; and Jo-Ann MacElhiney's indexing truly makes this a reference book.

And, as always, Robert Kuhn provided support of many kinds. I hope he knows how special his contribution to this book has been.